THE HOUSEHOLD OF FAITH

Notre Dame Studies in American Catholicism

Sponsored by the
Charles and Margaret Hall Cushwa Center
for the Study of American Catholicism

The Brownson-Hecker Correspondence
Joseph Gower and Richard Leliaert, editors

The Survival of American Innocence:
Catholicism in an Era of Disillusionment, 1920–1940
William M. Halsey

Faith and Fatherland:
The Polish Church War in Wisconsin, 1896–1918
Anthony J. Kuzniewski

Chicago's Catholics:
The Evolution of an American Identity
Charles Shanabruch

A Priest in Public Service:
Francis J. Haas and the New Deal
Thomas E. Blantz, C.S.C.

Corporation Sole:
Cardinal Mundelein and Chicago Catholicism
Edward R. Kantowicz

The Household of Faith

Roman Catholic Devotions
in Mid-Nineteenth-Century America

ANN TAVES

UNIVERSITY OF NOTRE DAME PRESS
NOTRE DAME, INDIANA 46556

Library of Congress Cataloging-in-Publication Data

Taves, Ann, 1952–
    The household of faith.

    Bibliography: p.
    Includes index.
    1. Devotional literature, English – History and
criticism.   2. Catholics – United States – Religious life.
I. Title.
BX2177.5.T38   1986   248.4'6'08822   85-41008
ISBN 0-268-01082-X

Contents

Preface

> The preacher must ... speak and act as though he were one of the audience, by addressing himself directly to God, to Jesus Christ, to His most Sacred Heart, to the Blessed Virgin on their behalf, by asking for mercy and forgiveness, and by forming appropriate resolutions. The people will naturally imitate the same sentiments in their hearts and make them their own.[1]

This quotation was taken from a handbook used by missionary priests in their efforts to transform the religious life of nineteenth-century American Catholics. It describes the technique used by these particular missionaries (Redemptorists) to create relationships between the lay people in their audiences and various religious figures, including God, Jesus Christ, the Sacred Heart of Jesus, and the Virgin Mary. The handbook encourages the preacher to model the desired relationship by addressing himself directly to these supernatural figures on behalf of his listeners. The passage also indicates something about the relationship between the preacher and his audience. The relationship is assumed to be such that the people will naturally imitate the preacher, thus reproducing the relationships modeled by him. If we define a culture as a network of relationships constituted by distinctive modes of interaction, then we may also view this handbook as a source which illuminates how a particular kind of Catholic culture was transmitted.

Although the source material available tells us more about what Catholic lay people were taught to do than about their responses, there is considerable evidence that forms of devotion new to English-speaking American Catholics were promoted and widely adopted during the mid-nineteenth century. Specifically, a range of evidence suggests that by the middle decades of the nineteenth century, the reception of the sacraments was overshadowed for most lay Catholics by devotional practices associated with Mary, Jesus, the Sacred Heart, and the Blessed Sacrament. In the chapters that follow, I will be concerned with the kind of Catholic culture that the promoters of such devotions intended to foster and, insofar as possible, lay response to its promotion. In this study, I will be using the image of "the household of faith" to describe the network of affective, familial relationships between believers and supernatural "relatives," such as Jesus and Mary, presupposed by the devotions.

A close analysis of the way in which such relationships were created and preserved will shed light on both the growing isolation of mid-nineteenth-century Catholics from the "mainstream" of American culture and the rapid institutional growth of the Catholic Church during this period. In contrast to the widely held belief that the shape of the American Catholic subculture was determined largely by the hostility of the Protestant majority, I will argue that mid-nineteenth-century Catholic missionary preachers, like Protestant evangelists of the same period, aggressively promoted an affectively oriented and sectarian, as opposed to ecumenical, form of piety intended to heighten the fervor of the laity and strengthen lay attachment to the institutional church. Moreover, I will suggest that the promotion of sectarian forms of piety by both Catholics and Protestants laid the groundwork for the creation and maintenance of separate institutional subcultures. This is not to say that hostility did not exist; rather it is to argue that hostility was exacerbated and used by both Catholics and Protestants in order to create and maintain their distinctive ways of life in a pluralistic and hence competitive environment.

This study will rely heavily on the devotional literature published in English for lay Catholic adults in the United States during the middle decades of the nineteenth century. As a didactic genre, devotional literature tells us more about the beliefs of those who wrote and promoted it than about those for whom it was intended. In the face of limited direct evidence regarding lay attitudes, I have sought to establish that the use of devotional literature increased sharply at mid-century and that the number and kinds of devotional practices increased in the more popular (better-selling) devotional books. I have supplemented this indirect evidence of increasing lay interest in devotional practices by examining letters written to the editors of the two most prominent nineteenth-century devotional magazines by their readers. Most of the letters suggest a belief in the miraculous efficacy of devotional practices.

In the first chapter, I will trace the emergence of a mass market for Catholic devotional books in the United States, indicate the ways in which they were disseminated, and examine the contexts in which such books were used. In the second chapter, I will document the proliferation of devotional practices in mid-century Catholic literature and begin a discussion of the worldview presupposed by these practices. The discussion of this worldview will be expanded in chapter 3 through an analysis of the accounts of miracles published in various American Catholic periodicals. In chapter 4, I will examine the more affectively oriented spirituality that underlay these devotional practices and explore the psychological roots of the affective bond between believers and supernatural patrons. In chapter 5, I will discuss why such devotions were promoted by the hierarchy and the way that this affective bond could be directed toward institutional as well as personal ends. In the final chapter, I will consider the effects of the rise of devotionalism on the formation of a Catholic subculture in the United States.

I have accumulated a number of debts in the process of preparing this manuscript. My friends Eileen Brewer, Scott Appleby, and Joseph McShane, S.J., provided the initial encouragement without which I might not have tackled a book on American Catholicism. Many others have been of assistance since. The reference staff of Regenstein Library at the University of Chicago cheerfully acquired copies of numerous hard-to-find nineteenth-century prayer books. Henry J. Bertels, S.J., of Georgetown University, provided information on several prayer books in the Woodstock Library collection. Joseph Chinnici, O.F.M., of the Graduate Theological Union in Berkeley, provided valuable criticism of an earlier version of chapters 1 and 2; Thomas Head, of the School of Theology at Claremont, provided helpful comments on chapter 3; both Bernard McGinn, of the University of Chicago, and a Catholic Studies Seminar at the University of Notre Dame provided helpful feedback on an earlier draft of chapter 4. Special thanks go to the reviewers whose thoughtful criticism of the manuscript aided enormously in the final revisions.

I would also like to thank the members of my dissertation committee at the University of Chicago: Martin E. Marty, who provided encouragement and intellectual stimulation throughout my graduate career; Bernard O. Brown, whose interests in ritual and social theory I stumbled upon with delight in his class on liturgy and society; and Jay Dolan, who, as an unofficial fourth reader, provided both critical comments and an enthusiastic interest in the subject matter which was greatly appreciated. The longstanding conviction of my advisor, Jerald Brauer, that to understand the religious life of a people one must begin with their piety, coupled with his interest in interdisciplinary approaches to the study of religion, provided a congenial starting point for my own research. Moreover, as an advisor, he consistently provided the sort of critical insight and emotional encouragement that can make a graduate education both exciting and humane.

Friends and family also provided generous assistance: Stephen Hoff provided both emotional support during the year and a half I was writing and an enormous amount of help with the University of Chicago computer system; Richard Poppen helped edit the entire manuscript for publication and suggested the new title, in addition to making the transition from a mainframe to a microcomputer almost painless; my colleague, Lynn Dumenil, helped with the proofreading; my research assistant, Gail Unterberger, did much of the work on the index; and my parents offered continuous encouragement throughout the process.

1

The Popularization of Devotional Literature

Although the centrality of the conversion experience in American Protestant piety has long been acknowledged, far less attention has been paid to the ongoing devotional life of those already converted. Charles Hambrick-Stowe has recently broken new ground in this area by using Puritan devotional manuals to focus on the practice of piety in seventeenth-century New England. In the course of his research Hambrick-Stowe discovered that Puritan devotional manuals shared much in common with their Catholic counterparts. In fact, according to Hambrick-Stowe, Puritans, recognizing "that Catholics were far ahead in this area," borrowed devotional techniques and verbal images, and adapted popular manuals, such as *The Imitation of Christ*, for Protestant use.[1]

Although Hambrick-Stowe's research points to the importance of this kind of devotional literature in both the Catholic and the Protestant traditions, little attention has been paid to its impact on religious life in America outside the Puritan context. Research on nineteenth-century evangelical Protestantism has focused on the relationship between religion and society, and neglected "the heartland of Evangelicalism," its inner spiritual life,[2] while research on nineteenth-century Catholicism has emphasized institutional history, episcopal biography, and the history of particular religious orders, again at the expense of the inner spiritual life of the church.[3] Writing in 1957, Henry F. Browne indicated that "little more than a plea has been made

1

toward a study of the devotional life of American Catholics including its Marian expressions."[4] Apart from the work of Jay Dolan, the situation has not improved dramatically since that time. Moreover, Dolan's work, while pioneering in its focus on lay Catholic piety, emphasizes the theme of conversion, particularly in the context of the parish mission, rather than the ongoing devotional life of the laity.[5]

PRINTING AND PIETY IN THE CATHOLIC TRADITION

In order to understand the impact of devotional literature on lay Catholics in mid-nineteenth century America, it is necessary to consider the impact of printing in general on the Catholic devotional tradition. Scholars generally recognize that the rise of printing played a crucial role in the shift from the medieval to the modern world.[6] Although its impact on the Protestant Reformation has generally been acknowledged, its impact on Roman Catholicism has been less frequently commented upon. Despite the fact that lay Bible reading did not play a prominent role in post-Tridentine Roman Catholicism, printing did have important effects on lay Catholic piety.

According to Jean Daniélou, "the invention of the printing press made it possible, for the first time in Christian history, to insist upon uniformity in worship." At the same time, the standardization of worship halted "all spontaneous growth and change" in the liturgy.[7] The standardization of the Mass in Latin thus sharpened the distinction between the liturgy and the paraliturgical practices, many of them in the vernacular, which existed alongside it.[8] Because the Mass was in Latin and thus not immediately interpretable by the ordinary lay person, the approved paraliturgical practices performed in conjunction with and in addition to the Mass took on special significance.

These approved practices were transmitted to the laity orally by seminary-trained secular clergy and the members of religious orders who conducted parish missions. They were transmitted textually by prayer books and devotional works. Although parish missions did not presuppose that the laity were literate, the missionary priests who conducted them were seminary-trained and relied upon printed manuals in order to communicate the spiritual disciplines of their religious orders to the laity.

In addition, however, the literate lay minority generated what was for the time an enormous demand for printed prayer books and works of devotion:

> By the end of the fifteenth century, not only had the production of prayer books become a profit-making urban enterprise, but supply for the first time seemed capable of meeting lay demand. A formidable task for hard-working copyists barely able to fill clerical markets had become a privilege keenly sought by printers who aimed at boosting sales.[9]

Moreover, the mysticism of the cloister and of localized movements, such as the *devotio moderna*, was popularized by means of the printing press. As a result,

> an extensive literature dealing with the interior life and intended for the use of people in the world as distinct from the cloister [emerged during the early and middle decades of the sixteenth century]. These range[d] from simple primers to sophisticated guides, mostly [written] by members of religious orders.[10]

Jean Delumeau's well-known thesis that "the average westerner [of the late Middle Ages] was but superficially christianized" attributes the "folklorization" of medieval Christianity to the ignorance of the secular clergy and the illiteracy of the mass of Christians, and presupposes that the transmission of (authentic) Catholicism required literacy and thus, I would add, was dramatically facilitated by printed books.[11] Although Delumeau reveals his theological predilections when he labels book-based Catholicism "Christianity" and folklorized Christianity a thinly veiled form of paganism, the distinction between book-based Catholicism, which depended for its transmission on an educated priesthood or an educated laity, and folk Catholicism, which did not, is an important one.

Although an educated lay elite generated a demand for prayer

books and works of devotion beginning as early as the late fifteenth century, mass education and cheap books were a product
of the nineteenth century. This meant that the book-based piety codified at Trent was taught to the majority of Catholics
orally, by preachers or educated secular clergy, until well into
the nineteenth century, and that where preachers and educated
secular clergy were unavailable or in short supply, the older forms
of piety were more likely to remain intact.

Because there were few if any parish missions and limited
numbers of educated secular priests in the English-speaking countries until the mid-nineteenth century, the spread of Tridentine-
style Catholicism was largely limited to an educated elite.[12] Although at the beginning of the nineteenth century illiteracy was
more widespread in rural Ireland than among Catholics in England and perhaps in the United States, the mass migration of
the Irish peasantry throughout the English-speaking world
heightened the disparities between educated and uneducated
Catholics in England and America as well. The increased opportunities for education during the peak period of Irish immigration, coupled with the introduction of English-language
parish missions and declining publishing costs, facilitated the
use of Catholic devotional literature by the laity.

THE EMERGENCE OF A MASS MARKET FOR BOOKS

Between 1830 and 1850, technological and social changes fostered the emergence of a mass market for books in the United
States. Changes in the printing process itself, introduced during the thirties, removed the physical barriers to mass produc-
tion that had previously existed. At the same time, the crusade
for literacy and mass education especially in the rapidly growing urban areas spurred book and magazine sales. The growing
demand for printed material at a price large numbers of people
could afford led to a publishing boom during the late forties
and fifties. In an attempt to meet the demand for inexpensive
books, many publishers, unhampered by an international copy-

right law, simply pirated European works.[13] An examination of Catholic devotional books published in the United States during this period suggests that these developments were reflected in the Catholic book trade as well.

In order to document this I examined prayer books and devotional guides published in English and intended for an adult lay audience. The former contained prayers, hymns, meditations, and instructions in the vernacular for all the ritual practices the lay Catholic was expected to perform. They were often used by the laity at Mass and other public services as well as for private devotions.[14] The latter contained prayers and instructions for the performance of one or two particular devotions. Devotional guides had titles such as *The Rosary and Scapular Book, Devout Practices in Honor of the Sacred Heart of Jesus,* and *The Sodality of the Blessed Virgin Mary.* They were often used by members of devotional organizations such as sodalities and confraternities.

Prayer Books

Four principal sources help us uncover America's long neglected nineteenth-century Catholic prayer books: Joseph Finotti's *Bibliographia Catholica Americana,* which lists books written by Catholic authors and published in the United States before 1820; Wilfrid Parsons' *Early Catholic Americana,* which lists books published in the United States between 1729 and 1830; John Wright's *Early Prayer Books of America,* which includes Catholic and non-Catholic prayer books published in North America before 1860; and a series of Master's theses from the Catholic University of America on nineteenth-century book publishing.[15] The lists included in these books were examined for prayer books published in the United States in English and intended for an adult lay Catholic audience. Prayer books obviously written for children were excluded. Publishers' advertisements in editions of *The Catholic Directory* were used to check the accuracy of the resulting list.

The final list includes 80 titles published prior to 1880 (see

Appendix A). Of these books, only 16 percent were introduced into the United States prior to 1830; the remainder, 84 percent, were introduced between 1830 and 1880. More than 30 percent of the prayer books appeared on the market for the first time during the 1850s (see Table 1). Most of the prayer books were English or Irish in origin.[16]

Devotional Guides

Tabulation of the devotional guides[17] listed in the Catholic University's *Survey of Catholic Book Publishing* indicates that the number published rose sharply during the fifties (see Table 2) reflecting the growing demand for devotional literature. Of 130 such books published between 1830 and 1880, only 9 percent were published between 1830 and 1850; the remaining 91 percent were published between 1850 and 1880. Because many of the guides were published anonymously, the country of origin could only be established for about half of the guides tabulated (see Table 3). Of those titles, 36 percent originated in England, Ireland, and the United States; 35 percent in France; and 16 percent in Italy.

In order to meet the increased demand for books, Catholic publishers, like their non-Catholic counterparts, turned to Europe. As a result, they were responsible for importing and, in many cases, translating large quantities of European devotional literature which was then sold cheaply on the American market.

TABLE 1

Prayer Books Introduced in U.S. by Decade, 1790–1880

pre-1800	4	1840–1849	15
1800–1809	4	1850–1859	25
1810–1819	3	1860–1869	12
1820–1829	2	1870–1879	4[a]
1830–1839	11		

[a] Since many of the prayer books introduced prior to 1870 were still being reissued, the drop in new titles introduced during the seventies probably reflected a declining need for new prayer books rather than a declining interest in prayer books.

TABLE 2

Devotional Guides Published in the U.S. by Decade, 1830–1880

1830–1839	3
1840–1849	9
1850–1859	51
1860–1869	30
1870–1879	37

TABLE 3

Devotional Guides by Country of Origin, 1830–1880

France	24	England	4
Italy	11	Ireland	4
Anglo-American	9[a]	Spain	3
United States	8	Austria	1
Germany	4	Netherlands	1

Total = 69

[a]Works in English of indeterminate origin.

The period from 1830 to 1860 was one of phenomenal growth for the church in the United States as well as for the publishing industry. Beginning with 318,000 Catholics in 1830, the Catholic population doubled approximately every decade to reach 3,103,000 by 1860. Of this increase of 2,785,000, approximately 69 percent was due to immigration, 28 percent to natural increase, 2 percent to conversion, and 0.1 percent to territorial expansion. The growth due to natural increase and conversion may be presumed to have added largely to the English-speaking Catholic population. Moreover, most of the immigrants were Irish and thus English-speaking as well. Of the 1,925,000 Catholics who immigrated between 1830 and 1860, about 1,300,000, or 67.5 percent, were Irish; 400,000, or 20.7 percent, were German; and 120,000, or 6.2 percent, were French.[18] In 1860 the Irish-born alone made up over one-third of the total Catholic population in the United States.

The publishing data suggest that the demand for devotional literature increased with, and roughly in proportion to, the growth of the English-speaking Catholic population in the United States.

If we assume that all Catholics were equally likely to buy and read books, such an observation would merit little consideration. In fact, however, prior to mid-century, both in the United States and in Ireland, book reading was limited to those with the means to buy books and the education necessary to read them.

As was the case more generally, changes in printing technology and literacy dramatically enlarged the market for Catholic books. The cost of Catholic books dropped rapidly over the course of the nineteenth century.[19] By mid-century, the price of a popular prayer book typically ranged between twenty-five cents and ten dollars, depending on the quality of the paper and the type of binding.[20] The drop in prices put book ownership within the range of the average American Catholic. Although, according to Soltow and Stevens, the ownership of more than three books was a sign of wealth at mid-century, "the ownership of from one to three books was common" and did not correlate with income.[21]

The demand for devotional literature was also stimulated by the growing availability of education. The common school movement, which greatly increased opportunities for elementary education, was at its height from about 1830 until the Civil War. The movement coincided with the years of peak Irish immigration and indeed was, at least in part, a response to the massive influx of immigrants.[22] Although early Catholic educational efforts were aimed primarily at an affluent lay elite, opportunities for a Catholic education at the elementary level also expanded during this period, largely in response to the growth of the common schools.[23]

In addition to increasing opportunities for formal schooling in the United States, many of the Irish immigrants had benefited from the establishment of a national system of public elementary schools in Ireland during the 1830s.[24] Instruction in the new schools was conducted in English rather than in Gaelic and thus facilitated the continued Anglicization of the Irish people. According to Donal Kerr, "the achievement of literacy in English by the majority of the [Irish] people was of first importance in spreading the new [Counter-Reformation] form of piety":

By 1848 over half a million children (mainly Catholic) were attending the national schools. As more and more people learned to read English, the new prayer-books became the staple devotional diet of Irish homes. Indeed the bundle that Paddy Leary took on his shoulder when he went off to Philadelphia almost certainly contained the *Garden of the Soul* or the *Key of Heaven*.[25]

As a result of the growing opportunities for schooling, illiteracy rates dropped in the northern United States from about 25 percent in 1800 to between 3 and 9 percent in 1840.[26] Access to education, however, did vary sharply with ethnicity and nativity, at least prior to 1850, according to Soltow and Stevens. By 1870, the differences between native and foreign born men[27] had decreased significantly and by 1890 there was little difference in the illiteracy rates between native and foreign born of either sex. There were, however, differences between particular ethnic groups, and Soltow and Stevens note that the illiteracy rate of 18 percent among male Irish immigrants in 1870 was particularly high.[28]

In a quantitative study of literacy in several mid-nineteenth-century Canadian cities, Harvey Graff also found that Irish Catholics "were over represented among the illiterate compared to their share of the total." Moreover, "their religion . . . importantly influenced their disadvantaged status, as the contrast with Protestants of Irish birth shows."[29] Graff goes on to point out, however, that

> the role of ethnic origins, and the disproportionate and undoubtedly highly visible place of the Irish and the Catholic among the illiterate, obscures one fundamental conclusion. Despite the facts of predominance and ethnic stratification, the great majority of the Irish were *literate:* in Hamilton [Ontario] only 20 percent of all Irish-born were illiterate, and estimates suggest a slightly lower rate in London and Kingston [Ontario]. Among Catholics, 70 percent were literate, as were 93 percent of the Protestants.[30]

These data suggest that by mid-century approximately 70 percent of all Irish Catholic immigrants had achieved at least minimal levels of literacy. Despite their low rate of literacy compared to the rest of the American population, the majority of Irish Catholic immigrants emerged during this period as actual or potential consumers of Catholic devotional books. In fact by the 1870s, it was apparent to one observer that the Catholic publishers' best customers were

> devout people of the poorer class, who have generally too little education to take an interest in literature, and for whom books of piety have to be manufactured in the cheapest possible way. Leave out this class of purchasers, the managers of schools, the clergy, and a few zealous and enlightened persons who make it a religious duty to buy numbers of good books to give away, and you will find that Catholic publishing houses have hardly any customers left.[31]

The rising demand for literature thus only incidentally coincided with the growth of the English-speaking Catholic population in the United States. In reality, it reflected dramatic shifts in publishing technology, literacy, and piety.

PARISH MISSIONS AND THE DISSEMINATION OF BOOKS

Mid-nineteenth-century Catholic publishers sold their books through two major outlets. The first was the canvasser or peddler who made the rounds of Catholic homes, schools, and churches. The second was the parish mission. Parish missions, like much of the piety they promoted, were not new. In their modern form they were instituted by orders of priests, such as the Barnabites, Capuchins, Oratorians, Vincentians, and Jesuits, during the sixteenth and early seventeenth centuries. The spirit of the parish mission, however, can probably be traced even further back to the popular preaching traditions inaugurated by the Franciscans and Dominicans in the thirteenth century.[32]

The impact of the parish mission varied in the centuries after the Council of Trent. Encouraged and influential during the seventeenth century, they were banned by many European governments during the late eighteenth century and only gradually reemerged during the nineteenth. During the nineteenth century, parish missions and the fervent piety they generated were most readily tolerated by monarchies which supported the church, e.g., France during the Restoration and the Second Empire, and by liberal regimes which constitutionally guaranteed the freedom of religion, e.g., Prussia between 1848 and 1870, the United States after 1789, and Great Britain after Emancipation in 1829.[33]

The aim of the parish mission was to revitalize the faith of the laity by inducing in them a desire for confession and communion, and an eagerness to persevere in the faith. To this end, participants assembled several times a day at the parish church for sermons and religious exercises conducted by a visiting missionary priest. Missions lasted from three to fourteen days; the longer missions were usually divided, the women attending the first week and the men the second.

Devotions, such as benediction of the Blessed Sacrament, corporate recitation of the rosary, the way of the cross, and the wearing of scapulars, were considered essential to the mission's goal of reviving and preserving the faith, and were frequently introduced into a parish for the first time by the mission preachers.[34] Devotional books and religious artifacts, such as rosaries, scapulars, statues, and holy pictures, which were used in conjunction with such practices, were sold at the parish missions.

Four religious orders – the Redemptorists, Paulists, Jesuits, and Passionists – gave most of the parish missions in the United States during the middle part of the nineteenth century. The Redemptorists began giving missions as early as 1832, but until 1851 almost all were in German or French. In 1851, they organized a trained band of full-time, American-born missionaries who devoted themselves exclusively to English-speaking congregations.[35] During the 1850s, the Redemptorists preached 188 missions, five times the number they had preached in the previous decade.[36] Moreover, during the fifties, the foreign-born Redemptorists began preaching increasing numbers of missions in English. In 1858, most of the American-born missionaries left the order to found the Paulists. Despite the loss, Redemptorists gave some 26 missions in English that year. In 1869, 62 out of 109 missions were given in English—well over 50 percent.[37] The Paulists continued to give missions to English-speaking parishes after they left the Redemptorists. Between 1858 and 1865, they preached some 81 missions.[38]

Like the Redemptorists, the earliest Jesuit missions were given mostly in German. Francis X. Weninger began full-time mission work among the Germans in 1848. During the mid-fifties, several Jesuits began giving missions to English-speaking congregations on a part-time basis. Father Damen of Holy Family parish in Chicago was the most important of these part-time preachers. In the early sixties, three other Jesuits joined Damen in preaching missions to English-speaking congregations in the midwest. In 1875, the eastern Jesuits fielded a team of six mission preachers as well.[39]

The Passionists began conducting missions in the churches of the diocese of Pittsburgh in 1856. Initially prohibited from traveling by the bishop, they did not begin giving missions outside the diocese until late in 1857. With a team of three preachers, they conducted 160 parish missions within the next decade in churches throughout the northeast and midwest.[40]

Both the total number of parish missions given in the United States and the percentage of missions given in English increased dramatically during the fifties and early sixties. With the introduction of itinerant preaching teams during this period, missions became a regular feature of parish life. Because most of the missions prior to that time were given in German, it is fair to conclude that English-speaking Catholics were largely unaffected by parish missions until the fifties.

The support of the bishops and local priests was essential to the spread of the parish mission movement. In 1866, at the Second Plenary Council of Baltimore, the bishops formally recognized the impact of the mission preachers. According to a contemporary report, the bishops described the missions as "one of the most efficacious means of procuring the salvation of souls." The council called for a house of missionaries to be founded in each diocese, for giving spiritual exercises in the parishes, above all during Lent, Advent, at the time of first communions, and the episcopal visitations. The parish priests are to co-operate cordially with these auxiliaries, and if any refuse to do so, they will be constrained by their bishops. On the other hand, all precautions are taken to avoid any appearance of interestedness, and any interference in the parochial government on the part of the missionaries.[41]

Prior to the Civil War, over-the-counter sales in bookstores were relatively small and thus parish missions in large city churches were an important source of sales. The competition for mission business was brisk.[42] Publishers offered special discounts on mission orders and promised to accept the return of all unsold goods. For example, in 1873, D. & J. Sadlier's, a Catholic publishing house, advertised a long list of articles it was prepared to supply, including rosaries, prayer books, bibles, devotional books, medals, crosses, crucifixes, statues, religious engravings, scapulars, holy water fonts, and lace pictures.[43]

Although mission preachers were sometimes accused of making money from these parish sales, the sales and the profits from them were apparently in the hands of the parish clergy. According to Father Damen,

> the pastor of the parish chooses some one to sell pious books, rosaries, medals, and other objects of piety and the profit from the sale is applied by the pastor to his church or school or to the poor. . . . The same thing is done in all the missions which are given by missionaries of other orders, the Redemptorists, the Lazarists, Passionists, Dominicans and all others. . . . The pastors and bishops want it absolutely and they take charge of it for the benefit of their churches and schools. To forbid it is to forbid the missions to our Fathers.[44]

Although intended primarily as a means of deepening the piety of the laity, parish missions also provided a source of income for the parish and a major sales outlet for Catholic publishers through the sale of books and religious artifacts promoted as essential to the devout Catholic life.

DEVOTIONAL ORGANIZATIONS AND BOOK USE

Parish-based confraternities and sodalities, intended to foster the devotional life of the ordinary Catholic, were often established in conjunction with parish missions. These organizations, which had names such as the Confraternity of the Blessed Sacrament or the Sodality of the Immaculate Conception, focused attention on one or more particular devotions. Many of the devotional guides were intended specifically for confraternity and sodality members, while others may have been used in that context as well. Many of these devotional organizations were responsible for establishing libraries either for the parish as a whole or for the members of their organizations. The sharp increase in the demand for books describing particular devotional practices, beginning in the fifties, probably reflected the rapid growth of parish-based devotional organizations at that time.

Prior to mid-century, parish-based confraternities and sodalities were quite rare both in the United States and in Ireland. According to Sean J. Connolly, the general level of religious practice among prefamine Irish Catholics was "more restricted in range and considerably less frequent" than in later decades. Although a few priests, especially in urban areas, were able to institute more elaborate devotions and "encourage . . . more frequent attendance at confession and communion through the establishment of lay societies and confraternities," such practices, while anticipating the major developments of the second half of the nineteenth century, did not, according to Connolly, "affect more than a minority of Irish Catholics."[45]

In the United States, as in Ireland, a few priests were able to anticipate developments which did not become general until later in the century. Such was the case with Charles Nerinckx, a missionary priest among the English-American Catholics of Kentucky, whose interest in parish organizations was, at least for the early nineteenth century, unusual. While still in Belgium, Nerinckx had experimented with parish organizations such as the Rosary Society, the Holy Name Society, and the Society for the Perpetual Adoration (of the Blessed Sacrament). Having experienced the devotional fervor which these organizations created among the laity, he obtained permission from Bishop Carroll to establish similar societies in Kentucky.

In an obituary notice printed in the *U. S. Catholic Miscellany*, Bishop Flaget of Bardstown stated:

> Nothing could exceed the devotion of Mr. Nerinckx to the Holy Sacrament of our altars; in this respect he was a model for every clergyman. In his churches, you saw only plainness except about the altar; but his devotion led him to aim at magnificence in this place, especially as regarded the tabernacle, which was to contain the Holy of Holies. . . . This good man had also great filial piety to Mary, the Mother of Jesus, and he desired to excite this affection in all those with whom he had any intercourse. . . . [To that end] he established the Society of the Holy Rosary, and the Confraternity and Sisterhood of the Scapular . . . in all the churches which he attended. . . . [Finally,] nothing could be more edifying than his piety toward the dead. It is impossible to pass by any of the numerous cemeteries which he has laid out, without deep sentiments of religion, and having a sweet sensation of deep melancholy, blended with the hope of the christian [sic]. In the midst of each abode of the dead is reared the glorious emblem of the christian's faith, a large cross, surrounded by a balustrade for the convenience of the pious friends who come to pray for their departed brethren.[46]

Probably the most active promoter of confraternities and sodalities during the first two decades of the century, Nerinckx even established babies' rosary societies. Martin Spalding, later archbishop of Baltimore, was enrolled in one of these societies in 1811 at St. Mary's church in Rolling Fork, Kentucky, at the age of one.[47] Some thirty years later, Spalding still remembered Nerinckx standing in the center of the church after Mass,

> where surrounded by the little children, who so dearly loved him, he knelt down, and, with his arms extended in the form of a cross, —the children raising also their little arms in the same manner— he recited prayers in honor of the five blessed wounds of our Divine Savior.[48]

As to the existence of pious organizations in other places comparable to those founded by Nerinckx, one of his biographers makes this comment:

> Such societies may have been already established in the older missions of Maryland, and probably some of them were in the better organized congregations, especially in the cities, but they were not general. Most of the priests had task enough trying to keep their own body and soul together at the same time, and besides, not all of them by any means had the zeal of Father Nerinckx.[49]

Although a few of the other societies to which Nerinckx's biographer referred were probably parish-based, early nineteenth-century devotional organizations were more commonly established in conjunction with elite academies and colleges. The first sodality in the United States was established at Georgetown College in about 1810. Other early sodalities were established in conjunction with convent schools, such as Georgetown Visitation in Washington, D.C., and the Convent of Mercy in New York City.[50] Through the establishment of these school-based confraternities and sodalities, elite academies and colleges encouraged the devotional life of their students and alumni. In them, wealth, education, and piety came together to generate much of the demand for devotional literature among lay Catholics during the early decades of the nineteenth century.

The growth of parish-based devotional organizations beginning at mid-century has been documented by the Parish History Project conducted by Jay P. Dolan and Jeffrey Burns at the University of Notre Dame. Their data, which include information on parish societies, were compiled from 980 parish histories from churches in forty states. Of these, 719 were founded prior to 1900.[51] The parish sample was heavily weighted toward the midwest, with parishes in Ohio, Indiana, Wisconsin, and Illinois making up 53 percent of the total. Because of its midwestern bias, the sample also contained a disproportionate number of German and rural parishes.[52]

Of the nineteenth-century parish organizations sampled, 60 percent were devotional; 26 percent were mutual aid; 6 percent, charitable; and 8 percent, miscellaneous other. The number of devotional organizations, as well as the total number of parish organizations, increased dramatically over time (see Table 4). Since all but 7 of the 719 parishes founded prior to 1900 were founded during the nineteenth century, this increase could simply have been a reflection of the increasing number of parishes. To check this, the number of devotional organizations founded prior to 1840 and prior to 1880 was divided by the number of parishes founded prior to 1840 and 1880, respectively. This revealed an increase from an average of 0.3 devotional organizations per parish in 1840 to an average of 0.7 in 1880, suggesting a substantial increase in the rate at which devotional organizations were established after 1840. If we assume that devotional organizations were distributed evenly (which is unlikely), then this would mean that 70 percent of all parishes had one devotional organization in 1880, compared with 30 percent in 1840.

Prior to 1900, the German parishes had almost twice as many devotional organizations per parish (1.5) as the English-speaking parishes (0.8).[53] Although a variety of factors might be considered to account for this difference, including the alleged German propensity to form organizations, two nonethnically related factors might also be considered. First, as indicated above, German-language parish missions began on a regular basis al-

TABLE 4

Types of Parish Organizations Founded, 1800–1900

Year Organization Founded	Total	Devotional	Mutual Aid	Charitable
1800–1820	2	1	1	0
1820–1840	24	18 (75%)[a]	2	3
1840–1860	151	108 (72%)	19 (13%)	14
1860–1880	395	240 (61%)	99 (25%)	27
1880–1900	756	427 (57%)	223 (29%)	41
1800–1900	1,328	794 (60%)	344 (26%)	85 (6%)

SOURCE: Compiled from data collected by Jay P. Dolan and Jeffrey Burns in conjunction with the Parish History Project at the University of Notre Dame.
[a] Percent of total number of groups founded during a given time period.

most two decades earlier than English-language parish missions. Second, 41 percent of all the German parishes, as compared with 18 percent of English-speaking parishes, were run by religious orders. German immigrants thus had greater exposure to the typically more intense piety of the religious orders, both in their parishes and through parish missions. Once English-language parish missions were begun on a large scale (after 1850), the percentage of devotional organizations founded in English-speaking parishes climbed rapidly.[54]

The project data also indicate that women made up the bulk of the members of the various devotional organizations. Prior to 1900, 60 percent of all devotional organizations were for women, 23.5 percent for men, 8.5 percent for men and women, and 8 percent for children (see Table 5).

While the increase in the overall number of Catholic devotional books published at mid-century reflected the rise of a mass market for books in general and Catholic devotional books in particular, the sharp increase in the demand for devotional guides beginning in the fifties coincided with the introduction of English-language parish missions and the rapid growth of devotional organizations in English-speaking parishes, suggesting that

TABLE 5

Devotional Organizations Founded, by Membership Groupings, 1800–1900

YEAR ORGANIZATION FOUNDED	TOTAL	WOMEN	MEN	MIXED	CHILDREN
1820–1840	18	11	5	2	0
1840–1860	108	65 (60%)[a]	30 (28%)	4 (4%)	9 (8%)
1860–1880	240	156 (65%)	53 (22%)	15 (6%)	16 (7%)
1880–1900	427	244 (60%)	99 (23%)	47 (11%)	37 (9%)
1820–1900	793	476 (60%)	187 (24%)	68 (9%)	62 (8%)

SOURCE: Compiled from data collected by Jay P. Dolan and Jeffrey Burns in conjunction with the Parish History Project at the University of Notre Dame.
[a] Percent of total founded during a given time period. Note: the figures given for women's groups include groups designated as being for women, single women, married women, and teenage girls; figures for men's groups include groups designated as being for men, married men, and teenage boys; figures for mixed groups included groups designated as mixed and teenage mixed.

these processes may have been linked. The growing demand for books indicates that by mid-century readership was no longer limited to a well-educated and predominantly English-American elite, but had been extended to include large numbers of literate, but not necessarily well-educated, Catholics as well. The immigration statistics would suggest that many, if not most, in this category were Irish immigrants or Americans of Irish descent, while the composition of the devotional organizations suggests that much of the demand for devotional books may have been generated by adult women.

2
The Rise of Devotionalism

An initial examination of a number of prayer books reveals that virtually every prayer book included prayers and instructions to be used in conjunction with the liturgical worship of the church. These included morning and evening prayer; instructions for hearing Mass; prayers to be said before, during, and after Mass; prayers and instructions for confession; prayers to be said before, during, and after communion; vespers for Sunday evening; prayers for the sick; and prayers for the dead. A number of traditional prayers, some of which were translations of prayers used in liturgical worship, were also included in almost every prayer book. These included the seven penitential psalms, the Litany of the Saints, the Jesus psalter, the prayer of St. Bernard to the Blessed Virgin, the Universal Prayer, the prayers of St. Bridget, and the "prayer for a woman with child."

Beyond this the content varied. Some contained little more than this basic material; others contained so much more that the basics seemed to be overshadowed. Devotions, along with more elaborate explanations of practices, made up most of the additional material in the larger prayer books. In order to investigate whether changes in the content of the prayer books varied over time, it is necessary first to define a "devotion" more carefully and then, in view of the number of prayer books published during the nineteenth century, to isolate the best-selling prayer books for detailed analysis.

DEFINING DEVOTIONS

The prayer books, because of their varied contents and their sometimes close relationship to the liturgy, raise the problem of distinguishing between devotions, the liturgy, and liturgically related actions.

The liturgy, according to Donald Attwater, can be defined as

> the forms of prayer, acts and ceremonies used in the public and official worship of the Church, principally in the offering of the Eucharistic Sacrifice, the singing of the Divine Office and the administration of the Sacraments.[1]

Although some prayer books included the text of the Mass with a translation, most contained only prayers and instructions for practices which could be performed either in conjunction with liturgical worship or separately. Their contents were thus mostly paraliturgical.

Attwater defines "popular devotions" as

> spontaneous movements of the Christian body toward this or that aspect of the faith, sanctified individual, or historical event, approved by authority and usually expressed in authorized vernacular formulas and observances.[2]

An advocate of liturgical reform, Attwater comments that "such devotions . . . have a somewhat disproportionate part in the lives of many." He indicates that although they have been approved and encouraged by church authorities, this approval and encouragement must be distinquished from "the solemn obligation which the Church imposes on clergy and laity in varying degrees to make use of her official public worship."[3]

Although Attwater probably would have liked to have been able to make a simple distinction between the public liturgical worship of the church and the private paraliturgical devotions of individuals, he admits that "popular devotions are susceptible of use in public as well as private." In fact, he indicates that it was "the introduction of these exercises . . . as a regular feature of church services" and hence the blurring of the distinction between the public liturgical worship of the church and the private devotions of individuals that gave rise to the twentieth-century liturgical movement.[4]

Since both the liturgy and devotions could be performed publicly and privately,[5] two other distinctions might better be emphasized: (1) the liturgy was in Latin, while devotions were "usually expressed in authorized vernacular formulas or observances," and (2) clergy and laity were obligated "in varying degrees to make use of . . . official public worship," while participation in devotions was voluntary, though recommended.

Attwater's definition of devotions as "movements . . . toward this or that aspect of the faith, sanctified individual, or historical event" does not include everything in the prayer books that could be considered paraliturgical. Robert Broderick, who uses the term "paraliturgical actions" rather than "popular devotions," defines the former more broadly to include all "those actions that are not strictly a part of liturgy proper but associated with it to a greater or lesser degree." He then differentiates between two "grades" of paraliturgical actions:

> (1) those that are an extension of the administration of the sacraments, for example, exposition of the Blessed Sacrament (Eucharist); scriptural or prayer devotions joined to the administration of a sacrament, such as Penance; (2) those devotions that may be done privately or in a group, and among these would be classified the recitation of the rosary, the Stations of the Cross, retreats (in their various forms), and novenas.[6]

Although Broderick's attempt to distinguish between two grades of paraliturgical devotions is helpful, I would define the categories somewhat differently. In the first category, I would include prayers in the vernacular to be used by the laity in conjunction with the liturgy, i.e., following Attwater, in conjunction with the Mass, the divine office, and the sacraments. This category would include morning and evening prayer and prayers for Mass, confession, communion, and confirmation.

I would not, however, include Blessed Sacrament devotions in this category, because, although they were theologically related to the doctrine of the real presence, they had little more to do with the sacraments in practice than did, for example, the rosary.

In the second category, I would include the "spontaneous movements of the Christian body towards this or that aspect of the faith [including the Blessed Sacrament], sanctified individual, or historical event, approved by authority and usually expressed in authorized vernacular formulas and observances," i.e., what Attwater calls popular devotions and what I will later define more rigorously as generalized devotions.[7]

THE PROLIFERATION OF DEVOTIONS

In the absence of good statistical data on book sales before the end of the nineteenth century,[8] I have tabulated imprint dates to give an idea of the demand for, and hence the popularity of, the various prayer books.[9] The devotions in the most popular prayer books[10] are tabulated, and the results summarized as pre- or post-1840, based on the initial date of publication for general use in the United States, in Table 6.[11]

The table indicates that there was an increase in the number of devotions included in the most popular prayer books published for a lay audience after 1840. While virtually all of the popular prayer books included one or more versions of the rosary and most included benediction of the Blessed Sacrament, prayer books published after 1840 were more likely to include other Marian devotions (e.g., the seven dolors, the Immaculate Conception, the Sacred Heart of Mary, and one or more scapulars) and other devotions to the Blessed Sacrament (e.g., the forty hours devotion and visits to the Blessed Sacrament) as well. Later prayer books were also more likely to include meditations on the passion as well as other devotions related to Jesus' passion, such as devotions to the Sacred Heart of Jesus, the way of the cross, happy death, the seven last words, the five wounds, and

TABLE 6

Devotions in the Most Popular Prayer Books, 1790–1880

DEVOTION	BEFORE 1840	AFTER 1840
Blessed Sacrament		
Benediction	9 (64%)	6 (75%)
Visits to	4 (29%)	7 (88%)
Forty hours devotion	0	5 (63%)
Mary		
Rosary (15-decade)	13 (93%)	8 (100%)
Other rosaries	9 (64%)	7 (88%)
Sacred Heart of Mary	4 (29%)	5 (63%)
Seven dolors of Mary	1 (07%)	5 (63%)
Immaculate Conception	1 (07%)	4 (50%)
Scapular (Mt. Carmel)	1 (07%)	6 (75%)
Other scapulars	0	3 (38%)
Jesus		
Sacred Heart of Jesus	6 (43%)	7 (88%)
Passion	4 (29%)	6 (75%)
Happy death	4 (29%)	7 (88%)
Agnus Dei	4 (29%)	5 (63%)
Crucifixion	3 (21%)	3 (38%)
Way of the cross	1 (07%)	7 (88%)
Infancy/childhood of Jesus	1 (07%)	4 (50%)
Saints, Souls		
St. Joseph	3 (21%)	7 (88%)
St. Aloysius	2 (14%)	5 (63%)
Souls in purgatory	1 (07%)	5 (63%)
Other		
Novenas	2 (14%)	4 (50%)
Litanies	1 (07%)	3 (38%)
Pious organizations	1 (07%)	3 (38%)
Special days of the week	4 (29%)	4 (50%)
Special months	0	1 (13%)

the Precious Blood. Novenas, litanies, devotions to St. Joseph, St. Aloysius, and the souls in purgatory were also more common in the later prayer books.

The devotions in the devotional guides[12] were basically the same as those found in the prayer books, with two significant exceptions – special months and the devotional organizations (see Table 7). Of the 51 guides published during the 1850s, seven provided prayers for the month of May, three for the month of June, and one for the month of November. During the 1860s

TABLE 7

Devotions in Devotional Guides by Decade, 1830–1880

DEVOTIONS	1830s	1840s	1850s	1860s	1870s
Blessed Sacrament	1	2	4	1	6
Jesus					
Sacred Heart	1		6	5	6
Passion/Lent/cross			7	2	3
Way of the cross			2		2
Happy death		1			
Sign of the cross					1
Mary					
Rosary		2	6	1	2
Mary (other)		1	2	1	3
Scapulars		2	7	1	2
Miraculous medal				1	
St. Joseph				1	2
Months					
May (Mary)	1		7	3	2
June (Sacred Heart)			3	3	1
March (St. Joseph)				3	1
January (infant Jesus)				1	
October (rosary)					1
November (souls in purgatory)			1		
Societies					
Confraternities		1	4	3	1
Sodalities		1	2	3	4
Other					
Novenas			4	2	2
Holy Family			1		
Trinity					1
Litanies					1

there were three more for May, three for June, three for March, and one for January. Each of the months was identified with a particular object of devotion—May with Mary, June with the Sacred Heart of Jesus or with the Precious Blood, March with Joseph, November with the souls in purgatory, and January with the holy infancy. Of the 130 books tabulated, eighteen (14 percent) were guides for sodalists or confraternity members. Many of the other books, particularly those on the rosary, scapulars, the Blessed Sacrament, and the Sacred Heart, were probably also intended for confraternity members.

THE CAUSES OF PROLIFERATION

Devotions proliferated in the devotional guides and most popular prayer books for a variety of reasons. The pope directly influenced the content of prayer books by granting indulgences for the recitation of specific prayers and the performance of specific rituals. Papal enthusiasm for granting indulgences rose and fell during the eighteenth and nineteenth centuries. After a period of decline, "a fresh impulse was given by Pius VI, which grew under Pius VII, and continued until Pius IX outstripped all his predecessors."[13]

Pius IX's zealous promotion of indulgenced devotions had an effect on both compilers and publishers of prayer books. As the number and importance of indulgences increased under Pius IX, compilers began marking the indulgenced prayers and informing their readers that the prayers had been literally translated from *The Raccolta*, the official handbook of indulgenced prayers. Publishers in turn passed this information on to consumers in the hope of selling more books.

D. & J. Sadlier, a New York publisher, included a lengthy quote from a book notice in the *Dublin Review* in their advertisement for the American edition of *The Golden Manual* which first appeared in this country in 1851. After noting the originality of the new prayer book and adding that "there is a certain sense in which this character would be any thing rather than a recommendation," the reviewer reassures his readers:

> The originality of the 'GOLDEN MANUAL' is of a perfectly unexceptional kind. It does not consist in the introduction of new and unauthorized prayers, or in the arbitrary and unsanctioned modification of old ones; but in the adjustment of the received prayers and devotional exercises in accordance with the best and most authentic usage, and particularly in adopting uniformly, and without exception, the form of each particular prayer, which had been approved by the Holy See, and to which an indulgence has been specially attached.[14]

The reviewer then notes that the editors of the *Golden Manual* added "a variety of most useful prayers and devotional exercises, which, though unknown to Catholics in [the British Isles], are, and long have been, familiar on the Continent. . . . In these also, especial attention had been paid to the devotions to which indulgences are attached."[15]

Similarly, numerous indulgenced devotions were added to *St. Vincent's Manual* when it was adapted for general lay use in the forties. According to a review in the *Pittsburg Catholic* [sic], which was quoted in Murphy's advertising, "additions [such] as the WAY OF THE CROSS, the prayers of BONA MORS, MEDITATIONS FOR EVERY DAY OF THE MONTH, the SCAPULAR, LIVING ROSARY, MONTH OF MARY, &c., give it that standard value that will make this the most popular of our excellent prayer books."[16]

Changes in the content of the prayer books occurred during a period of rapid growth in the Catholic population and coincided with the emergence of a mass market for books. Because less elaborate prayer books were available, the popularity of these devotion-laden prayer books was probably due at least in part to changes in taste and practice among the rapidly expanding Catholic population. At a minimum, the advertisements imply that the publishers considered numerous devotions and indulgenced prayers to be features which enhanced sales.

THE NATURE OF THE DEVOTIONS

In order to develop an understanding of the worldview presupposed by the prayer books and devotional guides, it is necessary to examine the devotions directly. The devotions in the prayer books and devotional guides had several features in common. First, many of the devotions were originally linked to particular religious orders. The forty hours devotion was originally associated with the Capuchins, the rosary with the Dominicans, the Sacred Heart and May devotions with the Jesuits, the way of the cross with the Franciscans, and the scapular with the Carmelites.

Second, all the devotions included in the prayer books were approved by church authorities. Most, although not all, of the

devotions had been granted papal indulgences and thus had acquired an authorized form which had to be followed in order
to gain the indulgences. Precisely what one had to do to gain
the indulgences varied from devotion to devotion. In some cases,
a particular prayer had to be recited, in others a particular action had to be performed. The instructions often allowed those
who could not read to recite a certain number of Our Fathers
or Hail Marys in place of reading the required prayer. The later prayer books tended to include more indulgenced devotions
and were more likely to make sure that their prayers and instructions followed the authorized form. This meant that the
devotions included in the prayer books were increasingly standardized.

Third, many of the most popular devotions were believed
to be supernaturally, as well as ecclesiastically, sanctioned. Many
of the devotions included in the approved prayer books, e.g.,
the forty hours devotion, the rosary, the scapulars, the Sacred
Heart, the miraculous medal, and the Immaculate Conception,
were accompanied by accounts of their origins which claimed
that they had been supernaturally instituted by miracles or visions. In many of these accounts, the founder of the devotion
received something from the supernatural patron in return for
his or her devotion.

Fourth, the devotions tended to be focused and specialized,
highlighting, as Attwater indicates, a particular "aspect of the
faith, sanctified individual, or historical event." The focused
and specialized character of the devotions meant that new devotions were continually being created to highlight different aspects of the faith. Although the variety of devotions can be con-
fusing to the uninitiated, they can be rather easily categorized
according to the object or type of devotion.

For the purposes of this discussion, the devotions will be
categorized either by subject: the Blessed Sacrament; Jesus; Mary;
Joseph, other saints, and the souls in purgatory; or by type: devotions for special months and days of the week, novenas, and
litanies. It should be noted, however, that the distinction between some of these categories is artificial. The devotions for

special months and days of the week, novenas, and litanies were all addressed to Jesus, Mary, the saints, or the Blessed Sacrament; moreover, devotions to the Blessed Sacrament were, in the Catholic mind, also devotions to Jesus. In analyzing the devotions, I will be concerned with the nature of the doctrines or images which they embodied, the kind of relationships between human and supernatural beings which they presupposed, and the context in which they were performed.

The Blessed Sacrament

Three devotions focused on the Blessed Sacrament: benediction, the forty hours devotion, and the practice of visiting the Blessed Sacrament. Veneration of the Blessed Sacrament was a devotional reflection of the Catholic doctrine of the real presence, which dated back to the twelfth century.[17]

Benediction was a public devotion in which Jesus, understood to be present in the consecrated wafer, was exposed to the adoration of the faithful and implored to bless those present before the altar.[18] According to Herbert Thurston, benediction of the Blessed Sacrament originated in certain short evening devotions to Mary, generally following Vespers or Compline, which became popular in the Middle Ages.[19] Prayers for benediction were usually included in the earliest American prayer books. Benediction usually followed Vespers on Sundays and holy days.[20] It was also celebrated during parish missions, sometimes as often as every day.[21]

The *forty hours devotion* was, as the name suggests, an exposition of the Blessed Sacrament for a period of forty hours in memory of the forty hours Jesus' body spent in the sepulchre. According to *The Mission Book*, the devotion originated with miraculous sanctions:

> In the year 1534, the city of Milan was suffering all the miseries attendant on war, . . . when [a Capuchin friar] called upon the citizens to . . . look up to heaven for succor, assuring them, on the part of God, that if they would give themselves to fervent prayer for forty hours, their city and their country would be liberated from

the devastations of their enemies. . . . The Forty Hours' Prayer commenced in the Cathedral, and was taken up by the other churches of the city in rotation. . . . Heaven did not delay to fulfil the assurance given by the pious servant of God; for in a short time the Emperor Charles V., and Francis, King of France, were seen at the gate of Milan arranging the articles of peace.[22]

The devotion became a means of expressing veneration for the Blessed Sacrament in the face of attacks on it by the church's "enemies." It was from this devotion that the idea of the "perpetual adoration" of the Blessed Sacrament developed.[23]

Although the forty hours devotion was not included in any of the early American prayer books, it was probably celebrated occasionally before mid-century.[24] John Neumann, a Redemptorist, is usually given credit for organizing and spreading this devotion in the United States. In 1853, while bishop of Philadelphia, he instituted the first schedule for observing this devotion in all the parishes of his diocese on a rotating basis. The system was intended to ensure that the sacrament was always exposed and venerated somewhere in the diocese.[25] The Second Plenary Council standardized the ritual used for this devotion and encouraged all bishops who had not set up scheduled diocesan devotions to do so.[26]

Visiting the Blessed Sacrament was an individual act of devotion for which lay persons were encouraged to set aside fifteen minutes or half an hour a day. While many books appeared in the post-Reformation period defending the Catholic practice of venerating the Blessed Sacrament and advocating devotional visits to it, the practice in its nineteenth-century form was popularized by St. Alphonsus Liguori in his book *Visits to the Blessed Sacrament*. During the fifties, Pius IX granted partial indulgences for reciting Liguori's prayers when visiting the Blessed Sacrament and a plenary indulgence for those who did so every day for a month.[27] As a result of these indulgences, Liguori's prayers were often incorporated in prayer books of the mid-fifties and beyond.

The central theme of Blessed Sacrament devotions was the adoration or veneration of Jesus' presence in the consecrated host.

In the face of attacks by "enemies," such adoration took on a protective or defensive quality which eventually gave rise to the practice of "perpetual adoration." In return for this constant adoration, devotees hoped and undoubtedly sometimes expected that Jesus would bless them and respond to their prayers, as he responded to the prayers of the Milanese.

Both benediction of the Blessed Sacrament and the forty hours devotion were corporate devotions. The former was often performed at the end of special days, including Sundays after Vespers, on holy days, and at the end of the day during parish missions. The latter was performed according to a year-round schedule set up by the bishops of a diocese. Thus, at times, it probably overlapped with, and perhaps obscured, more traditional aspects of the church year. Visits to the Blessed Sacrament were typically an individual act which could be scheduled at any time. Apart from unusual situations, Blessed Sacrament devotions were church-centered.

Jesus

Devotion to Jesus was directed toward his infancy and the passion. Devotions honoring the childhood and infancy of Jesus usually appeared in prayer books in the form of litanies and novenas, although prayers in other forms did appear, especially in the later prayer books. Devotions honoring Jesus' infancy and childhood were intended to focus attention on the mysteries of his incarnation and birth. Most of these devotions were associated with Christmas or the Advent season in general, although the twenty-fifth day of every month could also be devoted to the infancy of Jesus. Devotions honoring the infancy and childhood of Jesus were not indulgenced, except for the novenas, which were all indulgenced during the nineteenth century.

The passion-related devotions, including the fifteen meditations on the passion, the seven words of Jesus on the cross, the five wounds, the Precious Blood, the Bona Mors (happy death), the way of the cross, the Sacred Heart, the sign of the cross, and the Agnus Dei, appeared more frequently in the later prayer books. In general, the prayer books encouraged the laity to meditate on the passion in the context of the Mass.

Devotions which emphasized the details of the crucifixion, i.e., the seven words, the five wounds, and the Precious Blood, were all indulgenced during the first half of the nineteenth century and began appearing in prayer books after 1840.[28] Of themselves, these devotions were usually performed privately, often on Friday because of that day's association with the passion, and particularly on the Fridays of Lent. Passion meditations were, however, also an integral part of other devotions, such as the rosary, the chaplet of the five wounds, and the red scapular.

The object of the *Bona Mors* devotion was to obtain for oneself a "happy death." To secure this end, *St. Vincent's Manual* advised its readers "to honor the agony of Jesus expiring on the cross, and the martyrdom of his holy Mother on that tragic occasion."[29] Meditations on the five wounds often appeared among the sets of devotions recommended to ensure a happy death. There was also a confraternity associated with the Bona Mors devotion whose members were granted numerous indulgences. Jesuit missionaries were empowered to establish Bona Mors confraternities during the course of a parish mission.[30]

The *way of the cross* was a means of imitating a pilgrimage along the route of Jesus' passion in a parish church. The underlying belief in the value of pilgrimages to the sacred places of the Holy Land was very ancient. The idea of imitating the *via crucis* in a church was first promoted by the Dominicans and Franciscans during the Middle Ages.[31] Repeatedly promoted by various popes since the Council of Trent, this devotion had by the mid-eighteenth century acquired all the indulgences usually granted for an actual pilgrimage to the Holy Land.[32]

The way of the cross was usually performed in a church, in conjunction with pictures representing the events of the passion, although it could be performed at home using a crucifix specially indulgenced for that purpose.[33] Public performances were common during Lent and parish missions.[34] Prayers for this devotion, uncommon before 1840, were regularly included in prayer books published after that date.

The *Sacred Heart of Jesus* was typically pictured with a crown of thorns and a bleeding wound, both symbols of the passion. The bleeding wound was an outgrowth of devotion to the wound in Jesus' side. Though the symbolic connections between the heart as a source of blood and the heart as a source of love, both "spilled forth" at the crucifixion, were made during the Middle Ages, ritualized devotions to the Sacred Heart of Jesus did not begin until the sixteenth century.[35]

Seventeenth-century revelations to St. Margaret Mary Alacoque, a French nun in Paray-le-Monial, emphasized Jesus' love for humankind, symbolized in his bleeding heart, and the indifference, coldness, and ingratitude of most persons toward Jesus' presence in the Blessed Sacrament.[36] These two aspects of the devotion tended to merge in the mid-nineteenth-century prayer books. The result was devotion to and reparations for the Sacred Heart of Jesus present in the Blessed Sacrament.[37] In promoting June as the month of the Sacred Heart, an 1866 issue of the magazine *Ave Maria* stated that "the intention of all our readers during [June] should be reparation to the Holy Sacrament for the blasphemies of non-Catholics, and the coldness and indifference of bad Catholics."[38] Emerging from this identification of the Sacred Heart and the Blessed Sacrament was the idea of Jesus' presence as a voluntary "prisoner" in the eucharistic wafer. His continuing presence, understood as an extension of his life on earth, was perceived as a manifestation of his continued willingness to suffer out of love for humankind.[39]

Although devotion to the Sacred Heart had been practiced in the United States since the late eighteenth century, it was not until the 1870s, possibly due to the influence of additional missionary preachers as well as the Jesuit periodical *The Messenger of the Sacred Heart*, that the devotion was adopted widely.[40]

The *sign of the cross* was performed in both liturgical and extraliturgical contexts. Outside the liturgy, it was usually performed as a personal rather than as a corporate practice. Pius

IX granted the first indulgence for making the sign of the cross in 1863. He granted another in 1876 for making the sign of the cross with holy water.[41]

The *Agnus Dei* was a small cake of virgin wax stamped on one side with an image of the "Lamb of God immolated for us on the altar of the Cross." It was worn on the person, sometimes attached to a scapular. When properly blessed by the pope, it was believed to obtain for its wearer a number of benefits. While the Agnus Dei was not indulgenced, prayers to be recited daily by its wearers often appeared in prayer books after 1840.[42]

Devotion to Jesus centered on two themes: the incarnation and the passion. Of the two, passion-related devotions were far more prominent. The passion-related devotions emphasized Jesus' suffering by focusing on the details of the crucifixion. A number of devotions did this by elaborating on the biblical accounts of the crucifixion itself (i.e., the seven words, the five wounds, and the Precious Blood) or the passion more generally (e.g., the way of the cross). Others drew attention to the passion in a symbolic way (e.g., the Sacred Heart, the sign of the cross, and the Agnus Dei). Devotion to the Sacred Heart explicitly linked the ideas of suffering and love, while the connection between devotion to the Sacred Heart and devotion to the Blessed Sacrament linked the theme of suffering love with the theme of protective veneration in the face of hostility or indifference. Thus, Jesus, present on the altar, was viewed as loving and self-sacrificing, yet unappreciated, even abused, by many.

As a group, passion-related devotions were associated with Fridays, the Lenten season, and the Mass (where the host was consecrated). The way of the cross, the sign of the cross, and devotions to the Sacred Heart could all be performed corporately, as well as individually and in confraternities: the sign of the cross in the context of the liturgy, the way of the cross during Lent and at parish missions, and devotion to the Sacred Heart in the context of benediction or forty hours devotion. Passion-related devotions could be performed anywhere, but the association between passion meditations and the Mass and between Sacred Heart devotions and the Blessed Sacrament tended to make passion-devotions more church-centered.

Mary

Marian devotions included the rosary, the Immaculate Conception, the miraculous medal, the Sacred Heart of Mary, and most of the scapulars.

The *rosary* was a series of prayers counted on a string of beads, consisting of 150 Hail Marys and 15 Our Fathers, coupled with 15 meditations on the life and passion of Jesus. The practice of using beads as counters and the practice of reciting 150 Hail Marys in imitation of the 150 psalms of David both predate the thirteenth century. A form of the rosary similar to that practiced in the nineteenth century was introduced in the late fifteenth century by the Dominican Alan de Rupe and attributed to the founder of his order. The primary vehicle of its dissemination was the devotional confraternity.[43]

The rosary was included in all the most popular American prayer books. Although it was usually performed as a personal devotion, especially during the early nineteenth century, it could be performed corporately, and, by mid-century, often was, especially at parish missions and after Mass.[44] The rosary was well indulgenced by a series of popes, including Pius IX.[45]

Devotion to the *Immaculate Conception of Mary* predated the doctrine of the Immaculate Conception by many centuries. Popular veneration gave rise to the feast of the Immaculate Conception during the Middle Ages. Though many theologians rejected the doctrine of the Immaculate Conception, papal recognition of the feast of the Immaculate Conception during this period spurred efforts to gain recognition for the doctrine despite the opposition. These efforts did not bear fruit until the nineteenth century.[46]

Although Pius IX officially promulgated the doctrine of the Immaculate Conception in 1854, other factors, including the miraculous medal apparitions in 1830 and the Sixth Provincial Council's decision to make the Immaculate Conception the patronal feast of the United States in 1846, fostered devotion to the Immaculate Conception as well.[47] The apparition of Mary as the Immaculate Conception at Lourdes in 1858 was interpreted by many as a ratification of the papal decree and further fueled the fires of devotion. Devotion to the Immaculate Conception could be expressed through novenas and litanies or by wearing the blue scapular or the miraculous medal.

The *miraculous medal* was revealed by Mary to Catherine Labouré, a French nun, in a vision in 1830. On one side, the medal depicted the Virgin standing on a globe, crushing a serpent beneath her foot. Rays of light emanated from her outstretched hands. The words "O Mary, conceived without sin, pray for us who have recourse to thee" were inscribed around the figure. The other side depicted the hearts of Jesus and Mary, the one crowned with thorns, the other pierced with a sword. The first medals were struck in 1832. After a canonical inquiry certified the supernatural origin and spiritual efficacy of the medal, it was approved by the pope in 1842.[48]

The *Sacred Heart of Mary*, like the Sacred Heart of Jesus, was mentioned occasionally in medieval mystical texts and emerged as the object of devotional practice in the sixteenth century. In 1805, Pius VII granted the faculty to celebrate the feast of the Most Pure Heart of Mary to all dioceses that requested it. In 1855, Pius IX approved an office and Mass of the "most pure heart of Mary" without imposing them upon the whole church.[49] While devotion to the Sacred Heart of Jesus was linked through the image of the "wounded heart" to Jesus' passion, devotion to the Sacred Heart of Mary was linked through the image of the "pure heart" to Mary's Immaculate Conception. Thus, by mid-century, prayers were often addressed to the "sacred and immaculate heart of Mary." Prayers to the Sacred Heart of Mary, uncommon before 1840, were frequently included in prayer books after that time.

"*String-scapulars*," as Herbert Thurston called them, originated as badges of membership in a confraternity. A much reduced version of the scapular traditionally worn by monks, the string-scapular consisted of two small pieces of woolen cloth

united by strings and worn over the shoulders.[50] Wearing a
scapular was a sign of devotion to Mary, or, less frequently, to
Jesus, depending on the color of the scapular. Numerous benefits were thought to be attached to wearing a string-scapular.

Nineteenth-century prayer books date the origins of the brown
Carmelite scapular to an appearance of Mary to the monk Simon
Stock in a vision in 1265. According to tradition, "the blessed
Virgin appeared to him holding in her hand the form of a Scapular, and directed him to institute a pious confraternity, the members of which would consecrate themselves to her service, and
wear her livery" with the promise that those who did so would
"not suffer eternal fire."[51]

The "Sabbatine Bull," which according to tradition was promulgated by Pope John XXII in 1322 in response to a promise
made to him by the Virgin in a vision, contained the declara-
tion that those who wear the scapular will be promptly released
from purgatory on the first Saturday after death.[52] The Sabbatine Privilege was repeatedly promulgated by the popes of
the sixteenth and seventeenth centuries "in order to teach the
legitimacy of the doctrine of indulgences and of Marian devotion."[53] The historical authenticity of both the scapular promise to Simon Stock and the Sabbatine bull have been in question since the beginning of the twentieth century.[54]

In addition to the brown scapular of our Lady of Mount
Carmel, there were four other scapulars—the black scapular of
our Lady of Sorrows, associated with the Servites; the blue scapular of the Immaculate Conception, associated with the Theatines; the white scapular of the Trinity, associated with the
Trinitarians; and the red scapular of the passion of our Lord
Jesus Christ and of the Sacred Hearts of Jesus and Mary, associated with the Lazarists. These other scapulars were all popularized after the brown scapular, and according to Thurston,
"there seems to be no attempt to assign them to any earlier period than the seventeenth century."[55] The black, blue, and white
scapulars were often sewn together with the brown in order to
combine their benefits. The red scapular, revealed to a Sister
of Charity in a vision in 1846 and approved by Pius IX in 1847,

was worn separately.[56] Missionary orders were generally granted the faculties to bless the different scapulars, and made the distribution of scapulars a regular part of parish missions.[57]

Marian devotions focused on Mary as simultaneous symbol of purity (virgin, immaculately conceived) and fertility (motherhood) and as grace-filled mediator. Several important devotions approved at mid-century, including the Immaculate Conception of Mary, the miraculous medal ("Mary, conceived without sin"), and the Sacred ("most pure") Heart of Mary, emphasized Mary's purity. The scapulars highlighted Mary's intercessory power, especially at the time of death.

The rosary could be recited both corporately and individually. Lay people were encouraged to say the rosary (which included meditations on the passion) while hearing Mass. Scapulars and other devotional objects were commonly blessed at parish missions, although in general their use was a sign of personal devotion or membership in a confraternity. Corporate devotion to the Immaculate Conception and the Sacred Heart of Mary was associated with their respective feast days. Most Marian devotions could be performed anywhere. The popularity of Marian scapulars and medals and the portability of rosaries meant that Marian devotions, more than others, were associated with the person, rather than with the group.

St. Joseph, Other Saints, and the Souls in Purgatory

Private devotion to *St. Joseph* emerged in the West in the Middle Ages. The feast of the patronage of St. Joseph was extended to the whole church by Pius IX in 1847. In 1870, he gave further encouragement to the cult of St. Joseph by declaring him the patron of the Catholic Church and elevating his feast day.[58] Devotions to St. Joseph, rare in early prayer books, were almost always present in later ones. Devotion to St. Joseph was associated not only with his feast day, March 19, but also with the entire month of March.

Aloysius Gonzaga (often referred to as "the angelic youth") was a Jesuit noted for his studiousness and purity, who died at an early age. As a saint, he became the official patron of the young, but also, perhaps less formally, of students. Prayers to St. Aloysius for purity, to be recited at an altar dedicated to him on his feast day, were indulgenced during the eighteenth century, as was the "keeping" of six consecutive Sundays in his honor, apparently with pious meditations and prayers.[59] Prayers to St. Aloysius were much more common in the later prayer books.

One of the more important devotions to the *souls in purgatory*, described as a "heroic act of charity," was:

> A voluntary offering made to them, by any one of the faithful, of all works of satisfaction done by him in his life, as well as of all those which shall be offered for him after his death; placing them in the hands of the blessed Virgin, that she may distribute them in behalf of those souls whom it is her good pleasure to deliver from the pains of purgatory.[60]

This devotion was well indulgenced by several eighteenth- and nineteenth-century popes, including Pius IX.[61] Although prayers for the dead appeared in most of the prayer books, specific devotions for the souls in purgatory appeared with much greater frequency in later ones.

Special Months and Days of the Week

The dedication of May to the Virgin Mary, the first month to be singled out for a particular devotion, was inaugurated by the Jesuits during the eighteenth century.[62] May devotions were introduced into American parishes during the 1840s and spread rapidly thereafter.[63] Devotions to Mary were usually performed in a church, before a statue of Mary decorated with flowers. Some churches conducted formal devotions throughout the month. Richard Burtsell reports that "each evening [during May] . . . we have the Litanies, a short instruction, and a hymn."[64] May devotions were indulgenced by Pius VII in 1822 and again by Pius IX in 1859.

The idea of dedicating May to the Virgin was extended by analogy to other months of the year. Although every month came to be associated with a devotion, not all were equally popular. After May, the next most popular devotional months were March and June. In 1855, Piux IX granted indulgences for the dedication of March to St. Joseph. In 1850, he granted indulgences for the consecration of June to the Precious Blood, and in 1873 for the consecration of the same month to the Sacred Heart of Jesus.[65] The dedication of November to the souls in purgatory, October to the rosary, and January to the infancy of Jesus were apparently somewhat less popular.

The association of particular devotions with the various months of the year intensified the traditional identification of particular devotions with the days of the week. After Sunday, the most important days were Thursday, associated with the Blessed Sacrament; Friday, associated with the passion; and Saturday, associated with the Virgin Mary. Although prayer books often included prayers for the days of the week, more elaborate practices, such as the dedication of the first Friday of every month to the Sacred Heart of Jesus, did not become popular until late in the nineteenth century.

Novenas and Litanies

Novenas, which began appearing in prayer books after 1840, were associated with the various feasts of the church year. The purpose of a novena was to obtain a particular request through the intercession of the honoree. Novenas were performed both as corporate, public devotions and as private devotions for the nine days preceding the feast day of the mystery, saint, or aspect of Mary being honored. The devotional novena, a product of the popular piety of the Middle Ages, was not officially promoted until the nineteenth century. Early in the century Pius VII granted indulgences for novenas honoring Mary on her various feast days, and in 1849, Pius IX granted plenary indulgences for fifteen more novenas addressed to various saints and angels in addition to Jesus and Mary.[66]

Litanies, like novenas, appeared more often in prayer books after 1840. According to A. A. Lambing:

The invention of printing has often aided the mistaken and imprudent zeal of not a few, who have multiplied litanies without end, and gained for many of them a place in the endless number and variety of prayer books which flood the market. To restrain this pious weakness for manufacturing litanies—some of them not even free from heresy—the Sacred Congregation of Rites issued a decree, March 31, 1821, strictly forbidding any additions to be made to the litanies approved by the Holy See or the recitation of others in public that were not approved by the ordinary.[67]

The two litanies approved for public functions—the Litany of the Saints and the Litany of the Blessed Virgin—both had a traditional place in the worship life of the church. The Litany of the Saints was part of the liturgy, while the Litany of the Blessed Virgin, also known as the Litany of Loretto, was often used in May devotions. In private devotions, the Litany of the Blessed Virgin was often used to conclude the recitation of the rosary, and if done daily, five plenary indulgences per year were granted for this practice.[68] Although the prayer books that included additional litanies did not give many details about how they were to be used, it appears that they were to be recited privately on the feast day of the honoree or in conjunction with a novena just prior to the feast day.[69]

THE WORLDVIEW OF THE PRAYER BOOKS

Although devotions were, from a strictly liturgical point of view, peripheral to the life of the church at mid-century, the devotional literature suggests that they were central to the religious life of the laity. Because the Mass was in Latin, the vernacular prayer books provided lenses through which the laity could view the Mass. While some prayer books provided a translation of the Latin text, most included "devotions for Mass"— that is, prayers to be read while the Mass was celebrated—as well as various alternative methods for "hearing" or "assisting at" Mass. Devotions, particularly passion meditations and the rosary, were highly recommended means of assisting at Mass. *The Mission Book*, for example, states:

> In order to have a part in the merits of the holy Sacrifice of the Mass, either you must follow the actions and prayers of the Priest, especially at the three principal points; namely, at the Offertory, the Consecration and the Communion; or make a meditation upon the passion of Christ; or you may make use of devout prayers as you find them in your prayer books; or you may say the Rosary-beads in the mean while; or, in fine, make use of any other devout exercise best suited to your own feelings of devotion, uniting all the while your intention to the intention of the sacrificing priest.[70]

Although Richard Burtsell, a New York priest, personally favored a vernacular Mass, he included notes in his diary from a lecture on "Catholic Ceremonial" by a Jesuit, Father O'Connor, who valued the use of Latin in the liturgy because it preserved the distinction between the priest and the laity, and gave lay persons the freedom to pray according to their own inclinations:

> [O'Connor] would not use the usual argument that the faithful have the translation: he did not at all consider it necessary, or useful that the faithful should recite the same prayers as the priest, for the part of the priest is to sacrifice: the part of the faithful is to adore and to pray to Jesus there present: and it is better for them to have other prayers according to their dispositions of joy or melancholy from trouble. In Protestant service the people must follow in prayer the leader's sentiments and have no opportunity to pray according to their present dispositions.[71]

This discontinuity between the worship of the priest and the worship of the laity, although criticized by advocates of liturgical reform, lasted until well into the twentieth century. Writing in the 1920s, K. F. McMurtrie stated:

> At the present day it has become very common for the laity to take very little active part indeed in the official prayers and ceremonies of the Church. Thus at holy Mass you will commonly find the congregation engaged in all kinds of private devotions—recitation

of the Rosary, reading the so-called "devotions for Mass" provided in popular prayer books – devotions which are very different from the actual Mass-prayers themselves, and so on. Very few indeed are actually following carefully all the prayers and ceremonies of the holy Sacrifice as it is being enacted at the altar.[72]

Under the influence of the liturgical movement, descriptions of devotional practices became increasingly critical. Despite the critical tone, the following comments by Louis Bouyer illustrate how important these devotions actually were in shaping lay perceptions of the Mass:

> The popular devotion to the Child Jesus, the Way of the Cross (following the stages of the Passion but with no reminder of the Resurrection), and, later on, the devotion to the Blessed Sacrament thought of as a kind of substitute for Our Lord's sensible presence during the days of his earthly life, – all these were certainly so many developments at least foreign to the spirit of the liturgy, and often unconsciously but all too easily adopted in complete opposition to it. . . .
>
> We can see now that these novelties were able to take hold of the minds of the faithful so successfully because the liturgy itself had lost its hold upon them. Moreover, their very success made it more difficult to reestablish a true understanding and practice of the liturgy, since these new devotions involved a mentality not only foreign to that of the liturgy but almost irreconcilable with it.[73]

Liturgical reformers also complained that devotions distorted lay perceptions of the liturgical calendar. As they pointed out, the performance of a novena for nine days prior to a feast day or the performance of devotions to Joseph, Mary, the Sacred Heart, and the souls in purgatory on particular days of the week or for the entire months of March, May, June, and November could obscure liturgical seasons, such as Advent and Lent.[74]

If we disregard the normative agenda of the liturgical reformers, their observations provide a helpful entrée into the worldview of the nineteenth-century prayer books and devotional guides. First, there was discontinuity between the worship of the clergy and the laity in the context of the Mass, reflected in the clergy's use of the Latin missal and the laity's use of vernacular prayer books. Lay worship at Mass could be highly individualized, although both the prayer books and McMurtrie's remarks suggest that it was commonly centered on the consecration of the host, meditations on the passion, and the recitation of the rosary. Second, outside the context of the Mass, devotions were performed both individually and corporately. The corporate performance of a devotion, such as the rosary, benediction of the Blessed Sacrament, the forty hours devotion, the way of the cross, or May devotions, overcame the *formal* discontinuity between the religious practice of clergy and laity. (We can assume that some subjective discontinuity is present in all corporate activities.) Third, individual and corporate devotions gave a distinctive shape to the church year. Particular days of the week and months of the year took on devotional significance. Feast days, as well as the nine days leading up to them, were also unusually important.

The devotions themselves tended to involve both prayers and devotional objects such as the eucharistic wafer, scapulars, medals, holy water, and crucifixes. The prayers in the devotional literature were most commonly directed toward Jesus and Mary. In them, Jesus was usually portrayed as suffering out of love (in the passion-related devotions and in devotion to his Sacred Heart) and present in the face of hostility and indifference (in the Blessed Sacrament devotions). Mary was most often portrayed as pure (in the Immaculate Conception and Sacred Heart devotions) and protective (in the rosary and scapular devotions).

3
This World
and the Other World

Prayers to Mary and the saints in heaven and to Jesus in the
Blessed Sacrament presupposed a realistic and familiar relationship between the believer and the supernatural being to whom
the believer prayed. Devotions, in other words, presupposed the
existence of social relationships between faithful Catholics and
supernatural beings, and provided a means of interacting with
them. In his description of the bond between Christians and
their "invisible companions" in late antiquity, Peter Brown suggests that the saints filled a "need for intimacy with a protector
with whom one could identify as a fellow human being." The
particular qualities of the relationship were, he indicates, elabo-
rated in light of "known human relations between patron and
client."[1] While old interpretive metaphors lived on in the
nineteenth-century devotional literature, new metaphors emerged
as well. The bourgeois family or household in which the mother
played such a prominent role was frequently used as a metaphor
for the relationships between Catholics and the inhabitants of
the other world.

In exploring the nature of these relationships and the uses
to which they were put, it will become apparent that devotions
and devotional objects could be used for both spiritual and temporal ends. The tension between these two ways of entering into
devotional relationships emerges particularly clearly in the columns of the devotional magazines devoted to reports of the "graces
and favors" received in response to prayers. These columns sug-

gest that many lay people were more interested in receiving temporal benefits from their supernatural "relatives," than they were in receiving spiritual ones.

The Household of Faith

According to Isaac Hecker, "it is the sense of the nearness of the spiritual world, . . . pervading as it does the public worship, the private devotions, and the general tone of Catholics, that characterizes them from [Protestants]."[2] F. W. Faber makes a similar point in *All For Jesus* when he observes:

> What strikes heretics as so very portentous about us [is that] . . . we talk of the other world as if it was a city we were familiar with from long residence; just as we might talk of Paris, Brussels, or Berlin. We are not stopped by death. Sight of it is nothing to us; we go beyond it as calmly as possible. We are not separated from our dead. We know the saints a great deal better than if we had lived with them upon earth. We talk to the angels in their different choirs, as if they were, as they are, our brothers in Christ. . . . The blessed Lord God is our Father; His dear Majesty is our affair; our Elder Brother created us, and has our own nature; Mary is our mother; the angels and saints are all the kindest and most familiar of brothers; so we go up and down stairs, in and out, and to each other's rooms, just as it may be; there is no constraint about it at all; the air of the place is simply an intense filial love of the Father whom we all adore; so that our reverence is a children's reverence, and our fear a children's fear. . . . We use beads, medals, crucifixes, holy water, indulgences, sacraments, sacrifices, for all this, as naturally as pen, ink, and paper, or axe and saw, or spade and rake, for our earthly work.[3]

Faber provides us with an elaborately constructed image of the household of faith. Within this household everyone takes on a familial role: God is the father; Mary, the mother; and Jesus, the elder brother to all the angels, saints, and other Catholics, both living and dead. According to Orestes Brownson, one is born into this family through baptism:

All . . . who have been regenerated, born anew as begotten by the Holy Ghost, have the right to call Mary *Mother*, and our Lord himself *Brother*. . . . All of us who are born again in Baptism, the sacrament of regeneration, and [who] love our Lord Jesus Christ, are really and truly children of Mary, and she is really and truly our mother.[4]

Defending "the efforts of earnest priests and devout women to extend and intensify devotion to Mary, as the mother of God, and as our own dear and loving Mother," Brownson explains that for those "who believe in life eternal and the communion of saints . . . the holy ones in heaven [are] living and present with us." Like Faber, he emphasizes the intimate relationships which are possible between living and dead Catholics:

Death has not removed them from us. . . . They are present to our hearts, and we can speak to them, pour into their open and sympathizing hearts our joys and griefs, and ask and receive their aid, as readily and as effectively as when they were present to our bodily senses.[5]

The idea that the "holy ones in heaven [are] living and present with us" rests, as Brownson points out, on the doctrine of the communion of saints. Leo XIII defines the communion of saints as "a mutual communication" between "those who have reached heaven, or who are in the cleansing fire, or who are still pilgrims on the way in this world." This communication involves the sharing of "help, satisfaction, prayer, and other good works" such that all the faithful "come together to form one living city whose Head is Christ, and whose law is love."[6] Similarly, J. F. Sollier, writing for the 1908 edition of the *Catholic Encyclopedia*, describes the communion of saints as "the spiritual solidarity which binds together the faithful on earth, the souls in purgatory, and the saints in heaven in the organic unity of the same mystical body under Christ its head, and in a constant interchange of supernatural offices." This "mutual interchange" includes the sharing of "examples, prayers, merits, and satisfactions" within the earthly church and the sharing of "suffrages, invocation, intercession, [and] veneration" between "the Church on earth . . . and purgatory and heaven."[7]

The definition of the communion of saints offered by Leo XIII and developed by J. F. Sollier emphasizes the "mutual sharing" and "spiritual solidarity" which bound together faithful Catholics both living and dead. In these passages Leo XIII and Sollier replace the metaphor of the household with the metaphor of the city and the body, respectively. Thus, Leo XIII refers to the "one living city whose Head is Christ"; Sollier refers to "the mystical body under Christ its head." All three metaphors, however, suggest a complex, interdependent, whole dependent on mutual interchange and sharing for its survival. This sharing "in which everything belongs to everybody" is, according to Faber, "one of the most divine and striking characteristics of the communion of saints" and indeed, he claims, "of the Catholic religion."[8]

While the emphasis on sharing and solidarity highlights the dynamic character of these distinctively Catholic interactions, the use of household, city, and body metaphors for the church (in this world and the next) focuses attention on the role of those interactions in creating and maintaining the whole. Faber makes this connection explicit when he uses the body metaphor to observe that merits and prayers are interchanged "just as the blood circulates from and to the heart all over the body."[9] These dynamic interchanges, like the circulation of the blood in the body, were considered essential to the life of the church. Insofar as devotions were means of interchanging merits, prayers, and satisfactions; interceding for souls in purgatory; and venerating Jesus, Mary, and the saints; they facilitated the circulation of the sacred substance that kept the body alive. They were, to extend Faber's metaphor, the blood vessels of the body of Christ.

Technical discussions of the actual "substance" that was circulated often shifted to an economic metaphor, referring to "a treasury of sacred goods" which could be "exchanged." Theologians over the centuries described the contents of the treasury in a variety of ways. During the medieval period, its contents were sometimes said to consist of merits, sometimes of passions, and sometimes of satisfactions. One medieval theologian argued that the contents should properly be referred to as "superfluous satisfactions." Nor was there agreement as to whose merits, passions, or satisfactions made up the treasure. Some said those of Christ alone; others, Christ and the saints; others Christ, the Virgin, and all the apostles, martyrs and saints, living and dead.[10]

Since the Council of Trent did not resolve the matter, nineteenth-century theologians tended to describe the treasure as consisting of the merits and satisfactions of both Christ and the saints and sometimes those of the Virgin as well.[11] The description in *St. Vincent's Manual* was typical:

> The merits and satisfaction of Jesus Christ are of infinite value; they can never be exhausted. . . . The merits and satisfaction of the Saints . . . have their value from Jesus Christ . . . [and] so, by the communion which all the members of Jesus Christ's mystical body have with one another, [they] are applicable to the faithful on earth.[12]

For our purposes it is enough to say that the treasury was filled with vaguely defined benefits or power derived in some way from the superabundant holiness of Jesus, the saints, and Mary. These benefits could be dispensed by God in the form of graces and favors, or by the hierarchy in the form of indulgences. Devotions played an integral part in the acquisition of the benefits. Just as by analogy to the body, devotions could be viewed as the "vessels" through which the sacred substance "flowed," so by analogy to a gift economy, devotions could be viewed as the "occasions" on which people could expect to "receive" benefits.[13]

GRACES AND FAVORS

The prayer books indicate that Catholics could expect to receive graces and favors from God through Jesus and Mary as well as indulgences authorized by the pope when they performed devotions. The prayer books suggest that some devotions and some ways of performing devotions were thought to be more effective means of acquiring graces and favors than others.

The most efficacious, at least from the perspective of the prayer books, were those petitions for graces and favors made to God in the presence of the consecrated host, whether at Mass, at communion, or reserved on the altar. A number of the more popular prayer books reminded their readers that petitions made during the Mass were the equivalent of prayers offered at the foot of the cross. *The Ursuline Manual* asks its readers if they would "have hesitated in asking *any favour* . . . had [they] been at the foot of the Cross" and instructs them to "be firmly convinced that [their] confidence in God should be equally lively whenever [they] hear Mass." The manual encourages them to "ask for any thing and every thing [they] desire" during Mass, for Jesus' "sacred blood and infinite merits plead your cause just as efficaciously on the altar as they did on Mount Calvary."[14]

The period following communion was also thought to be an auspicious time to obtain favors from Jesus. According to *The Catholic Manual*, "it is then Jesus Christ plentifully lavishes his choicest favours on those who are careful to collect them."[15] Moreover, according to *The Mission Book*, Jesus "remains on our altars . . . [in order] to dispense his graces to us, and to show us his love." The manual encourages its readers to "converse familiarly with Jesus . . . implor[ing] his pardon for all [their] offenses, lay[ing] before him all [their] wants, as one friend does to another in whom he places all his confidence."[16] According to *St. Vincent's Manual*, visiting Jesus on the altar is one of "the most effectual means of nourishing in our heart the love of God, and of strengthening ourselves against the occasions of sin" and encourages its readers to "spend a few moments daily in the presence of your Saviour, to invoke upon yourself and yours his blessing, and the graces you have need of."[17]

Devotional practices related to Mary were also touted as especially efficacious means of acquiring graces and favors. *St. Vincent's Manual* claimed that "the Rosary, when said with proper dispositions, is a powerful means to obtain favor from God."

The manual pointed out that many "public favors" and "private graces" had been obtained in this way and encouraged its readers to see for themselves, asserting that "experience itself will soon convince all, who apply to it in earnest, how powerful a means it is to obtain our petitions from the Almighty."[18] Similarly, *The Ursuline Manual*, in its instructions for saying the rosary, encouraged its readers to excite the proper sentiments of devotion by thinking "of the consolation it will be to you on your death-bed, to have said your Beads devoutly, and thereby implored, upwards of fifty times every day, the assistance of the Blessed Virgin for that dreadful hour."[19] Moreover, "by saying [the Our Father in the rosary] in a proper disposition you can please God more, and obtain more graces, than if you were to run through all the books of devotion that were ever written."[20]

The Mission Book also assured its readers that Mary would obtain for them "great graces in return for the little acts of love and homage" which they offered to her. In this regard, the prayer book particularly encouraged them "not to neglect those devotions which are so well approved, and so generally practiced by devout Catholics, such as the Visits to the Blessed Virgin, the Litany [of Loretto], and the Rosary."[21]

Novenas, according to *The Ursuline Manual*, could be made "in honour of some mystery of our Redemption, to obtain a particular request; or in honour of the Blessed Virgin, or any of the Saints, to beg their intercession in obtaining a favour from God."[22] "Religious souls," according to *Ave Maria*, "prepare themselves to celebrate great festivals by practices of devotion [such as novenas], because they know that on these solemn days divine favors are diffused more abundantly on hearts well prepared. . . . " Assuming that its readers usually made novenas in preparation for Marian feasts, the article urged them to consider a novena in preparation for the feast day of St. Joseph on the grounds that "such homage is singularly agreeable to him, and obliges him to accord extraordinary favors reserved for his faithful servants, as experience makes us believe."[23]

Some devotions were set up in such a way that the devotee benefited from the merits earned by others. "The Living Rosary," for example, allowed a circle of fifteen people to divide up the task of saying the rosary. Although each member had to recite only one decade each day, every member received "the full merit of the entire Rosary recited by the circle."[24] Those who wore scapulars were entitled to even greater benefits. According to *The Mission Book*, those who wore this miniature habit were entitled to "a share in all the masses, prayers, almsdeeds, penances and other good works continually offered to God in the Religious Orders [i.e., the Carmelites, Servites, Theatines, etc.] represented by the Scapulars."[25]

Although the prayer books make it clear that devotions were a means of receiving graces and favors, they were usually quite vague when it came to explaining exactly what graces or favors one should pray for. In a rare enumeration of particular graces and favors for which the reader might pray, in this instance at Mass, *The Ursuline Manual* suggests:

> [Prayers] to obtain the grace to conquer some fault; to acquire some virtue; for the conversion of some sinner; for those who are in the agonies of death; or for the suffering of the souls in purgatory. . . .[26]

Examination of devotional magazines and novels of the period suggests that devotions were not performed only for the sort of spiritual graces and favors suggested by *The Ursuline Manual*. In the context of late nineteenth-century American Catholic fiction, Paul Messbarger concluded:

> The Catholic who [said] the rosary daily, who [made] the nine First Fridays, or who [prayed] to St. Anthony, [could] expect anything, from protection against physical harm to reconciliation with an estranged husband or material success. Thus, in one short story an army sergeant who has fallen away from the Church, wears from habit a badge of the Sacred Heart and is by that gesture led back to the Faith. In another story, a boy who is about to succumb to the temptation of drink is, because he has made the nine First Fridays, given the grace to resist. A prayer to St. Anthony leads to the discovery of a lost waif. A medal of the Blessed Virgin protects a Civil War soldier from the effects of a bullet.[27]

The same kinds of stories, with perhaps more emphasis on the rosary, scapular, and Sacred Heart, and less on St. Anthony or the first Fridays, recur in the fiction published in *Ave Maria* and *The Messenger of the Sacred Heart* between 1865 and 1880. Moreover, the same kinds of stories appear in the *non*fiction columns as well.

Both *Ave Maria* and *The Messenger of the Sacred Heart* sponsored devotional organizations — *Ave Maria* supported the Confraternity of the Immaculate Conception and the Association of Our Lady of the Sacred Heart; *The Messenger of the Sacred Heart* supported the Apostolate of Prayer. The purpose of these organizations was to pray as a group for the needs and requests submitted by their members. Both magazines published the prayer requests of their members, as well as columns detailing the "favors obtained" through prayer. Occasionally they published fairly long letters from their readers or reprinted from Catholic newspapers detailing particularly spectacular "favors."

The most varied lists of "favors obtained" generally gave the fewest details. The following is a typical excerpt from the "Graces Obtained" column of *The Messenger of the Sacred Heart*:

> Thanks are returned for the cure of a young man who had been for a long time a partial cripple; also for the reform of the father of a family formerly addicted to intemperance.
>
> I desire to return thanks for the conversion of a friend for whom prayers were asked last year.
>
> It has pleased God to call to Himself my dear mother by a most holy and happy death, a grace for which she often asked the prayers of the Apostleship.
>
> Tender and heartfelt thanksgivings for the wonderful and unexpected recovery of one recommended last month; also for the perseverance of a young man who has been doing very well since he was by the merciful Heart of Jesus claimed from an irregular life.
>
> Thanks to the Sacred Heart for graces received.
>
> We thank the Sacred Heart for many graces obtained, v.g. the success of a mission, increase in a sodality and signs of conversion in an unfortunate woman.
>
> Through the mercy of the Divine Heart of Jesus my mother's mind has improved since she was recommended.
>
> Thanks are tendered for a young person's restoration to health. . . .
>
> Sincerely grateful to the Sacred Heart for favors received, I now ask, &c.

Request the Associates to offer ardent thanks to the Sacred Heart
for a special favor obtained at a time when its realization appeared
impossible.

Return thanks for the conversion to the Faith of a man recommended about a year ago; likewise for the reformation of two in-
ebriates and for the partial success of an undertaking attended with
many difficulties.

I desire to return heartfelt thanks for the favorable change
wrought in my husband since I asked prayers for him.[28]

Apart from unspecified favors, the most commonly reported
results of prayer were conversions; cures; resolution of family
difficulties; moral reform, particularly of the intemperate; and
happy deaths. Accounts in *Ave Maria* of "favors obtained" were
somewhat more heavily weighted toward cures than were those
in *The Messenger of the Sacred Heart*.[29] Moreover, in the more
extended reports in both magazines, accounts of conversions and
cures predominate.[30]

MIRACULOUS CURES AND OTHER TEMPORAL FAVORS

Like spiritual favors, miraculous cures and other temporal
favors were attributed to the intercessory powers of Jesus, Mary,
the saints, and fellow human beings. Although little compara-
tive work has been done on nineteenth-century healing traditions, miraculous cures do not appear to have been as common
in the United States as they were in traditionally Catholic countries or regions, such as France, Spain, Ireland, or Quebec. Certainly there were no shrines in the United States which rivaled
those at Lourdes and La Sallette in France, Knock in Ireland,
or Beaupré in Quebec.

Through mid-century, most American Protestants, or at least
most Protestant leaders, rejected the possibility of "modern miracles." By the latter decades of the nineteenth century, however,
"faith cures" had become increasingly common among a wide
spectrum of religious groups in the United States. James Monroe Buckley, editor of the Methodist *Christian Advocate*, indi-

rectly reveals the extent of the interest in miraculous healing when he attempts to debunk Protestant claims by pointing out that "in comparison with the Mormons, Spiritualists, Mind-Curers, Roman Catholics, and Magnetizers, the Protestant Faith-Healers can accomplish as much, but no more."[31] While many Protestant leaders maintained their skepticism, general interest in miraculous cures appears to have been very widespread both in the United States and Europe during the latter part of the nineteenth century.

The best known and most completely documented cure of an American Catholic took place on March 10, 1824, and illustrates the connections between the European and American Catholic healing traditions. The cure of Ann Mattingly, sister of an early nineteenth-century mayor of Washington, D.C., was credited to the intercessory powers of Prince Hohenlohe, a famed German healer and priest.[32] A pamphlet describing the miraculous cures of three British women by Prince Hohenlohe had been published in the United States less than a year before Mattingly was cured.[33] Hohenlohe effected these cures at a distance rather than in person by establishing specific times when he would offer intercessory prayers for people in different places. Those desiring to pray for someone living outside Europe were instructed to join with him in prayer at a specific time on the tenth day of any given month after completing a specific course of preparatory devotions. The prayers for Mattingly were coordinated by her priest, Rev. S. L. Dubuisson, who arranged, following the prince's instructions, for her relatives and close friends to perform a novena to the Holy Name of Jesus every morning at sunrise for the first nine days of the month. Shortly after the time the prince had agreed to pray for those living outside Europe, Mattingly, still following the prince's instructions, received communion. Soon after swallowing the host, she was, according to the accounts, cured of a disease which sounds from the descriptions like an advanced case of breast cancer.

Other cures were reported through the intercession of the Sacred Heart,[34] the Virgin Mary, and the saints. Like the cure of Ann Mattingly, most of these cures depended on sacred actions or objects which connected the American Catholic with sources of sacred power which originated in Europe. Thus, cures with the aid of Mary often involved holy water from Lourdes and sometimes La Sallette; the rosary; novenas; or medals, such as the miraculous medal or the medal of Our Lady of the Sacred Heart.[35]

Cures involving the water of Lourdes, distributed by *Ave Maria*, were particularly common.[36] According to a French priest traveling in the United States in the late 1870s, holy water in general played an important part in the devotional life of the Irish. They customarily "sprinkl[e] themselves several times with holy water on leaving the church . . . [and] frequently . . . fill a small phial from the contents of the font and carry it away with them as a precious treasure."[37] The respect accorded holy water stemmed from its protective and curative powers. According to this priest, "this *holy water* is an all-powerful arm with which the priest must be ever furnished when he goes to visit the sick among the Irish, for it is always their first and at times their most efficacious remedy." He then goes on to describe how an Irish man dying of cholera was cured with holy water.[38]

Other accounts indicate that Mary protected her devotees from accidental death as well as sickness. In one account, a husband wrote in to describe how his wife, sensing disaster, had their children "say an extra 'Hail Mary' . . . for protection." That night a water pipe burst "miraculously" and put out a fire which threatened to destroy both the house and its inhabitants.[39]

In another account, a Civil War officer wrote in to describe how his commander's life had been saved by the scapular he had been wearing. According to the letter, dated December 13, 1864, the commander, a Major General D. S. S———, was a recent convert and "a most devout Catholic" who prepared for the battle in question by making his confession to the Catholic chaplain in an open field in full view of his officers. During the battle that followed:

> A bullet entered [the commander's] coat on his right shoulder, and came out on his left; in passing from shoulder to shoulder, it tore

the flesh all along, except one spot about two inches wide upon which his Scapular rested. . . . When the battle was over, . . . the General showed me the Scapular, with one string cut and the end that was on his neck was bloody.

"This Scapular," said he, "was given to me last Easter by Father Cooney, and I believe it has saved my life. And," he added, "nothing in this world could buy it; I shall keep it as a precious relic as long as I live."[40]

According to the officer:

[The] little spot [where the scapular rested] covered the vertebra of the neck, at the head of the spinal column, which, if broken, would [have] cause[d] almost instant death. The surgeons decided that one quarter of an inch *lower* would have caused death, and the Scapular appears to have raised the range of the bullet at least that much.

The scapular, he concluded, "turned the bullet out of a straight line, to which it returned again, as if to make the power of God more manifest."[41]

Father Richard Burtsell, a priest in New York City during the 1860s, recorded the telling of a similar tale by one of his fellow priests during a talk on the scapular. In this case, however, the wearer is protected from death even though he was attempting to commit a mortal sin:

[Father Lancake] spoke at H. Mass on the Scapular: instituted by Simon Stock superior of the Carmelites, whose beginning dates back to the Apostles, and they were always remarkable for devotion to the B. Virgin. The B. Virgin promised that none should perish eternally who wore the scapular at the hour of death: he said that one who was to be damned would lay aside the scapular at that time, or before it. He had read of a man who sought to commit suicide by drowning, and after 5 attempts succeeded only when he took off the scapular.[42]

About a month later, Burtsell noted in his diary that "Fr. Lancake . . . spoke about the delusive piety of wearing scapulars etc. without avoiding sin."[43]

Cures with the aid of the saints usually involved relics which had been brought to the United States from Europe. Some mission preachers routinely carried relics with them and cures were reported on occasion at parish missions. Father Weninger, S.J., carried relics of Peter Claver with him and reportedly effected numerous cures, several of which aided in Claver's beatification.[44] The Passionists carried the relics of their founder, St. Paul of the Passion. Reports of cures at their mission in Brooklyn in 1857 brought a great deal of press coverage and renewed the discussions of "modern miracles" in the papers.[45]

Other accounts indicate that some mission preachers told stories of miraculous cures worked by relics located at particular shrines. In one such account, a middle-aged farmer took his elderly mother on a two-day journey to a convent in Kentucky "with a view of saying a novena before the shrine of Our Lady of Loretto, thereby to obtain the cure of her long standing affliction." The idea for such a cure had been planted in her mind by the priest who served as spiritual director for the order. According to the account, "it was he who, in one of his distant missions, had first informed the afflicted lady of the many marvelous cures that were operated before the altar of Our Lady of Loretto." While they were there, they stayed with a Mary C., a pious but skeptical woman who lived on the grounds of the convent. On informing the superior of the convent of the pilgrims' visit, Mrs. C. comments: "Poor old lady, one foot in the grave and the other on its brink, expecting a miracle to cure her old age." The superior, however, took the request seriously, and she and some of the sisters began a novena at the bedside of the paralyzed woman.

According to the account, prayers were offered before a relic of St. Francis de Hieronymo. At the close of the prayer, "to which the sick lady had responded with piety, fervor, devotion, and faith," she was given the relic to kiss. After a brief exhortation, the sister applied the relic to her head. At that point, according to the account:

The closed dull eye of the sick woman immediately moved, opened and brightened; then as the relic was moved to the shoulder, the arm, the side, down to the feet, and touched each member, life, health, strength, motion, flexibility were all communicated. . . . [Then] with the elasticity of youth, she arose from her bed, and threw herself upon her knees to thank Our Dear Lady and Saint Francis for this marvelous favor.[46]

Mrs. C., who had concealed herself so as "not to give offense by her mirth," had an immediate change of heart. At the sight of the miracle, "fear of the judgement of God stole over her, and she experienced a deep remorse for amusing herself over holy things."[47]

Skeptical Catholics, such as Mrs. C., recur in other accounts. Robert A. Bakewell, a St. Louis lawyer, wrote a letter to the *Freeman's Journal* describing both the miraculous cure of his daughter's hip disease with a relic of Sophie Barat and his own skeptical reaction. According to Bakewell, his wife, "who was almost worn out with broken sleep and anxiety" because of their daughter's illness, called upon the Sisters of the Sacred Heart for help without his knowledge. The sisters gave her a relic of Barat, the founder of their order, and informed her that "fourteen miracles had already been worked by her relics."

Bakewell's wife "applied" the relic that evening and by the next morning the child was cured. Bakewell, of course, was skeptical. In response to her tearful announcement, Bakewell recounts:

I told my wife not to allow herself to give way to a false impression. . . . The chances, I said, are ten millions to one that you have mistaken some natural symptom of the disease which caused the temporary cessation of pain for a cure. My wife left me in disgust; my airs of superior wisdom having no other effect upon her, as far as I could see.[48]

Bakewell then made similar remarks to his daughter. Sitting upon her bed, he "resumed [his] lecture, adding many sage reflections." According to Bakewell:

The little girl heard me patiently, and when I was quite through, merely said: "But, papa, I am cured." Her assurance surprised me. I told her to get up and walk then, which she did at once, standing, for some seconds, at my request, on the right leg alone. I then told her to go to bed and stay there till the doctor came to see her. . . . Dr. Gregory examined the child last night, and pronounced her entirely cured, and said to me on leaving the house: "You have my authority for saying that Cissey's was the most clearly developed case of incipient hip disease that ever I saw in my whole practice."[49]

These accounts suggest that miraculous cures were usually associated both with devotional acts, such as novenas, confession, communion, or prayers to Mary and the saints, and with devotional objects that were believed to have or transmit supernatural power, such as eucharistic wafers, scapulars, or relics. Whether the object's power should be attributed to God, Jesus, Mary, or a saint, or was believed to inhere in the object itself, was not of central importance in these accounts. These stories, actual accounts of miracles, were less concerned with how miracles happened than with convincing skeptics, including Catholic skeptics, that miracles were happening. The primary concern of these stories, in other words, was to witness to the action of the supernatural in this world.

Accounts of modern miracles reinforced the Catholic's belief in the nearness of the other world, sanctioning both the believer's faith in and mode of communication with the supernatural inhabitants of that supernatural world. Like medieval miracles, modern miracles projected,

> in however distant and confused a way, an image of men within the household of faith. . . . In this context, the miracles of the saints were simply the ordinary life of heaven made manifest in earthly affairs, chinks in the barriers between heaven and earth, a situation in which not to have miracles was a cause of surprise, terror, and dismay.[50]

This underlying sense of a household of faith which included both natural and supernatural members is revealed most clearly in the story of Archbishop Spalding's death, an occasion when prayers for a miraculous cure were not answered. According to Father Daniel E. Hudson, editor of *Ave Maria*, Spalding had written him shortly before his death and, at the end of the letter, "after mentioning the bad state of his health, . . . recommend[ed] himself to the prayers of the communities of Notre

Dame and St. Mary's." Although, according to the article, they and the thousands of others who prayed for the health of the archbishop "did not obtain the blessing [for which] they had fervently asked, their prayers were not unheard." According to Hudson, Mary responded to their prayers by appearing in person to Spalding on his deathbed.

A description of the incident is given by Louise Collins, the Sister of Charity who nursed Spalding during the last weeks of his life. According to Collins, the apparition occurred on a Sunday evening after they had prayed together:

> When we had finished, he continued to move his lips in silent prayer. All at once he raised his eyes and hands toward heaven, his countenance lighted up, and in an ecstacy of delight he exclaimed: "O my beautiful mother! my sweet mother! how beautiful thou art!" He said to me: "Oh! do you see her?" But all I saw was his countenance, so radiant that I know not how to describe it.

When she asked him what he had seen, he said:

> "Well, I will tell you, but you must say nothing of it, for the world would only laugh at it. My Blessed Mother has deigned to visit me, and I saw her Divine Son at a distance. She smiled on me, and said: 'Courage my child; all will be well; I will soon come again.' But she did not tell me when." Then looking at the pictures of the Blessed Virgin, he said: "Take them away; I can no longer see in them any trace of my beautiful Mother."[51]

Here the favor bestowed is not a cure but a personal encounter with Mary herself. Rather than simply a sign of the supernatural, in this case, a supernatural being actually appears in this world. In light of the apparitions at La Sallette and Lourdes, which had been well publicized in the American devotional magazines, such an appearance would not have been inconceivable.

The Uses of Miracles

There is no evidence that the publication of miracle stories in *Ave Maria* and *The Messenger of the Sacred Heart* created a great stir among the magazines' Catholic readers. Nor did that seem to be the intention of the editors. Rather, miracle stories were published to edify believers. They were intended to illustrate the efficacy of prayer and consequently to increase intercourse between this world and the other world.

The Messenger of the Sacred Heart stated that its lists of "graces obtained" were intended "to inspire and increase our confidence in the Heart of Jesus, and in the efficacy of united prayer, as also to increase the zeal of the members, and especially of the promoters of the Association of the Apostleship to spread it more and more."[52] *Ave Maria* printed the letter from the Civil War officer because "of the very edifying incidents it relates—additional developments of the Divine sanction to the practice of devotion to the Mother of God."[53] When the Bostonian wrote to describe how saying the rosary had saved his family from a fire, he explained that he thought "others might be edified in hearing of it, and thereby have their devotion to our dear Mother increased."[54]

Unlike medieval miracles, however, modern miracles had distinctly anti-Protestant overtones. The account of the cure of the elderly woman at the Convent of Loretto interpreted the miracle as another sign of the truth of Catholicism:

> How absurd the idea put forth by the Protestant world, that the age of miracles has passed away. . . . Has there ever been a period of the Church that has not been illustrated by miracles? History will answer: *No!* If then in our midst, in the clear light of heaven, in the presence of Catholic and Protestant, such favors are granted . . . can anyone be so bold as to deny . . . that [the Catholic Church] stands unmoved by the revolutions of ages which . . . have broken against the rock-built Church, only to display their utter impotency?[55]

Because most Protestant apologists rejected both the idea of modern miracles and the means which Catholics used to obtain them, all miracles recognized by nineteenth-century Catholics had inherent propaganda value. John Milner, an English bishop, felt that it was the "doctrines and practices, by means or in favour of which [miracles] have been wrought" which lay at the root of the Protestant rejection of modern miracles.[56] Most miracles, as Milner pointed out, were "connected with what [were] commonly called Popish superstitions, such as the sign of the cross, prayers to the saints, a veneration for their relics and pictures, prayers for the dead, the real presence, the sacrifice of the mass, &c."[57] Protestants thus knew, Milner claimed, that if they recognized modern miracles, they would also have to admit that the means by which they were wrought were "devoid of superstition, and even actually pleasing to the Almighty."[58]

Considering the difficulties involved in establishing that an event was a "real" as opposed to an apparent miracle, apart from an appeal to authority, the usefulness of Catholic propaganda was probably largely limited to those who already acknowledged the possibility of miracles – or better yet, the authority of the church to authenticate them.[59] Thus, as anti-Protestant propaganda, alleged miracles were undoubtedly most effective, first, among Catholics and, second, among those Protestants who were already disposed to believe in them.

Although *Ave Maria* and *The Messenger of the Sacred Heart* published reports of miraculous cures and other temporal favors for didactic and polemical reasons, they also published them to please their readers. People clearly liked to write in to these magazines to recount what God, or Jesus, or Mary had done for them or those for whom they had prayed. *The Messenger of the Sacred Heart* recognized this and acknowledged that it published readers' letters not only to increase members' confidence in the efficacy of prayer, but also "to gratify the pious desires of correspondents."[60]

THE VALUE OF MIRACLES

The fact that so many of *Ave Maria*'s readers wrote in to acknowledge temporal rather than spiritual favors provoked a comment from the editor, Father Daniel E. Hudson. Although, he acknowledged, "most of the favors we publish each week are temporal, . . . it would be wrong to assume that they are the only ones obtained through the intercession of the Blessed Virgin. Spiritual favors do not come so easily to our notice."[61] Hudson went on to justify the publication of such lists on the grounds that "the cures and other temporal benefits wrought through [Mary's] intercession are very often merely a means to prepare souls for favors of a higher order, conversion and sanctification."[62] Although the magazine's editor valued spiritual favors, such as conversion and sanctification, more highly than temporal favors, such as cures, he nevertheless promoted prayer as an efficacious means of gaining temporal benefits in order, it seems, to appeal to a wider audience.

While physical healing was of secondary importance to the editor, this was not necessarily the case for his readers. In fact the large number of letters acknowledging temporal favors suggests that this-worldly problems were the primary concern of many of the magazine's readers. Analysis of the miraculous cures attributed to the Passionist Fathers, both at their well-documented Brooklyn mission in 1857 and in the course of their settled ministry in Hoboken suggests that there were at least three different sorts of responses to reports of miraculous cures.

Non-Catholic reporters tended to respond to Catholic accounts of cures by requesting further documentation. A reporter from the New York *Sunday Mercury* visiting the Passionists at their monastery in West Hoboken in the 1870s asked for the names of people who had been cured. According to the article, Father Vitalian, the priest interviewed, responded:

> We don't keep any record of these people. We never ask their names or anything about them. The priest [blesses them with the relics], gives them certain prayers to say, and usually directs them to confession and Communion (if they have neglected it), but that is all. Our work goes on all the time, and we could not stop to inquire into every detail.[63]

Similarly, the *Commercial Advertiser of New York* responded to the *Freeman's Journal*'s account of the cures at the Brooklyn mission by asking "what pains [the Catholic paper] had taken to ascertain facts, dates, and names of the cured." The *Freeman's Journal*'s response was *"very little indeed!"*[64]

While both Father Vitalian and James McMaster, editor of the *Freeman's Journal*, believed that miracles, in the popular sense of the term,[65] had occurred, both refused to get very excited about them. Father Vitalian saw such healings as a normal part of his ministry:

> Everyday [he said] people come here [to the monastery in Hoboken] to be blessed with the relics, and go away again. Then after a while they come back to us and tell us what it has done for them, but not always. Sometimes one priest administers the blessing and sometimes another; but we generally hear from each other all that occurs. We don't talk about it to outsiders or make noise about it, for it is only part of God's work in His Church, and it does no good to publish it in the newspapers.[66]

McMaster also saw miracles as a normal part of the church's life. Like Hudson, he was less impressed with the cures than with the conversions that in some cases accompanied them. He pointed out that in the minds of non-Catholic journalists a miraculous cure "is a thing so unheard-of, unaccountable and next to impossible, that they would expect us to drop our ordinary duties of life on the instant and with note-book and pencil, rush over to Father Gaudentius [Rossi], like the reporter of a two-penny newspaper to the scene of a riot."[67] Since, as a Catholic, he knows "that [God] has promised the perpetual power of working miracles to the Catholic Church," he asserts that his belief in God's power to work miracles in the present "could not be strengthened were we to see a dead man restored to life, or one born dumb made to speak eloquently, every day in the year." For that reason, as well as reasons of "temperament and disposition" which he does not describe, McMaster states that "were Father Gaudentius to have continued for a year curing daily all manner of diseases in Brooklyn, with the relics of Blessed Paul of the Cross, it is not likely we would have gone to witness one of them." He argues that conversions are actually "a greater miracle, than the cure of all the bodily ailments" and claims that had he found time "to visit Brooklyn during that Mission, it would have been to hear Father Gaudentius preach, or to have met with him and his new converts in conversation, much rather than to have inquired the how and the where of the physical cures that were effected."[68]

Reports of the miraculous cures produced a different effect, however, on those who were sick. According to Yuhaus, records from the mission indicate that

> the sick . . . besieged the missionaries for prayers and blessings, stationing themselves at the door of the rectory and along the pathway to the church doors before either the church or the rectory was opened. When Fathers Calandri and Rossi came into view, suffering people "took hold of the missioners by the cloak or arm and with tears in their eyes asked to be blessed and cured. . . . The missioners having to go from the priests' house to the church had the greatest difficulty to free themselves from these importunities."[69]

Although the reporter who visited the Passionists in Hoboken almost twenty years later could not get from the fathers the name of anyone who had been cured, a mother did bring her daughter in to be cured while he was there. He interviewed the woman, a Mrs. Trahay from Brooklyn, who told him that her six-year-old daughter Maggie had St. Vitus' Dance. The woman had

> lost her confidence in doctors . . . and determined to look for other help. She had heard of the miracles wrought by the Passionist Fathers, and had heard that they had cured children of St. Vitus' Dance. On close questioning, Mrs. Trahay did not personally know any parties who had been healed, but she had met a good many who told her of these cases and she had every reason to believe it was all true.[70]

Finally, both reports indicate that the enthusiastic response of the sick to reports of miraculous cures was not limited to Catholics. The fact that Catholic apologists downplayed miracles relative to sanctification and Protestant apologists discounted the possibility of modern miracles altogether did not seem to keep the sick, Catholic or Protestant, from seeking cures.[71]

Examination of accounts of miraculous cures and other temporal favors suggests that such events could be, and were, perceived either as means to an end or as ends in themselves. Those who perceived them as means were primarily concerned with spiritual ends, such as conversion and sanctification; their ultimate goal was the salvation of souls. Those who perceived such events as ends in themselves were primarily concerned with temporal goals, such as health, personal safety, family harmony, or financial prosperity.[72]

Mid-nineteenth-century missionary preachers and devotional literature energetically promoted ties between the inhabitants of this world and the next. Explicitly and implicitly, they portrayed the Catholic's world as a "household of faith" in which human beings and their supernatural "relatives" could converse through prayer in an intimate and friendly manner. Devotions thus provided a means of communicating with these supernatural relatives, while devotional objects served to remind devotees and those around them of their commitment to such relationships. Within such a cosmos, the idea that devotional acts and objects might be associated with miraculous cures and apparitions did not come as a surprise. Miracles were simply tangible proof of the reality of the relationships that devotional acts and objects presupposed.

4

The Affective Bond

A resurgence of affective spirituality underlay the popularization of such a devotional cosmos. Two spiritual writers, Alphonsus Liguori and Frederick William Faber, exemplified this affective style. Liguori, an eighteenth-century Italian, was an important moral theologian, founder of the Redemptorists, and, as of the nineteenth century, a canonized saint. Faber, a nineteenth-century Englishman, was an Oxford convert, an Oratorian, and a contemporary of John Henry Newman. Both Liguori and Faber were missionary preachers, Liguori among rural Italians and Faber among London's immigrant Irish. Both were tremendously popular in the United States, and indeed throughout the Catholic world, during the middle decades of the nineteenth century.[1]

Both Liguori and Faber were indebted to Francis de Sales, a seventeenth-century Genevan bishop and author of the *Introduction to the Devout Life*, one of the first devotional works written specifically for the laity. Though all three addressed themselves to the needs of the laity, de Sales's *Introduction to the Devout Life*, unlike the writings of Liguori and Faber, placed little emphasis on devotions and was emotionally fairly restrained. In the English-speaking world, de Sales's more subdued style was typically associated with the upper-class English Catholicism of the post-Reformation period and with the early English immigrants to the American colonies. While this more restrained approach never died out, it was eclipsed during the mid-nineteenth century by the more emotional, devotion-oriented style asso-

ciated with writers such as Liguori and Faber and with ultra-
montanism more generally.

In an article comparing Protestant revivals and Catholic parish missions, Orestes Brownson admitted that in order to be
effective

> Religion must appeal to the heart, rouse the passions, strike on
> the senses, affect the sensibilities. It must awaken the popular mind,
> take hold strongly on masses of men, and be able to master and
> sway the wills, not only of the educated, but of the ignorant, the
> gross, the debased, and vicious even.[2]

He granted that "for a small class habituated to meditation . . .
a calm quiet retreat spent in solitude and silence, is more agreeable and more salutary" than an emotionally rousing parish mission. But, he continued,

> these are few; the majority, even of the higher and more educated
> class, can only take part in, and be benefited by, what are called
> *popular devotions*, and the only way of giving them the benefit of
> the spiritual exercises is by means of a parish mission.[3]

Francis de Sales's *Introduction to a Devout Life*, first published
in the United States in 1806,[4] reflected the spirituality of the
"calm quiet retreat." De Sales's influence was enhanced by *The
Garden of the Soul*, a prayer book written by Richard Challoner,
an eighteenth-century English bishop. Like de Sales's *Introduction*, *The Garden of the Soul* acknowledged the importance of
Mary and the saints, but did not give them much prominence;
it included only two devotions, benediction of the Blessed Sacrament and the rosary (see Appendix D).[5]

In the *Introduction to a Devout Life*, de Sales distinguishes
between an introductory set of ten meditations designed to prepare the initiate to choose to live a devout life and meditations
on the passion intended to form the basis for actually living a

devout life. The introductory meditations are on subjects such as creation, sin, death, heaven, and hell. In the last of the ten meditations the reader chooses between Jesus and the devil and, choosing the devout life, takes a place among the "band of devout souls" gathered around "Jesus Christ crucified."[6]

Although de Sales does not include specific instructions for meditation on the passion—he refers the reader to a number of other authors instead—it is clear that meditations on the passion pick up logically from where the ten-day meditation leaves off. In the passion meditations Jesus becomes the focus of and model for the devout life:

> By making him the frequent subject of your meditation, your whole soul will be replenished with him; you will imbibe his spirit, and frame all your actions according to the model of his. . . . In fine, as little children, by hearing their mothers talk, lisp at first, and learn at length to speak their language; so we, by keeping close to our Saviour by meditation, and observing his words, actions, and affections, shall, by the help of his grace, learn to speak, to act, and to will like him.[7]

A condensed version of the ten introductory meditations as well as de Sales's instructions on meditation or mental prayer were included in *The Garden of the Soul*.

While Liguori's devotional works were frequently reprinted after mid-century[8] his influence was also felt through the parish missions. Both the handbook used by the Redemptorists to conduct parish missions and *The Mission Book*, a popular mid-century prayer book, drew heavily from his writings. *The Mission Book*, first published in the United States in 1853, was frequently sold at parish missions. Unlike *The Garden of the Soul*, it contained numerous devotions designed to "preserve the fruits of the mission" (see Appendix D).[9]

The Redemptorists' handbook reveals the underlying structural similarity between their parish missions and the course of meditations prescribed by de Sales. The sermons used by the Redemptorists at parish missions were on topics such as penance, salvation, mortal sin, confession, death, general judgment, hell, the mercy of God, the passion of Christ, the blessed Virgin Mary, and the means of perseverance.[10] Apart from the sermon on perseverance, the topics for the mission sermons correspond quite closely to the topics which de Sales covered in his introductory set of ten meditations. Like de Sales's meditations, the Redemptorists' sermons were designed to impress the hearer with the consequences of sin, the threat of damnation, and the opportunity for salvation through the mercy of God. Moreover, both were intended to persuade the participant to make a choice between a life of piety and a life of sin.[11]

Like de Sales's instructions for daily meditation on the passion, the mission sermons on perseverance, which included sermons on avoiding the proximate occasion of sin, the necessity and efficacy of prayer, and the importance of holy communion, provided instructions for Christians attempting to lead a devout life in the world. *The Mission Book*, which was advertised as a "means of preserving the fruits of the mission," expanded on the sermons on perseverance by providing a number of passion-related devotions in an expanded prayer book format.

MEDITATION

Despite these structural similarities, there were important differences in their understanding of meditation. Specifically, where de Sales attempted to direct emotions generated by meditation into ethical action, more affectively oriented spiritual writers, such as Liguori and Faber, used meditations to form affective bonds between human and supernatural beings.

The method of meditation[12] which de Sales outlines is a simplified version of the Ignatian method consisting of three parts: the preparation, the meditation proper, and the conclusion. The crucial section, for our purposes, is the meditation proper, which is also made up of three parts: considerations, affections, and resolutions. The considerations, according to de Sales, are acts of the intellect which "raise up our affections to God."[13] These considerations in turn produce pious emotions in the will, or affective part of our soul: such as the love of God and our neighbor; a desire of heaven and eternal glory; zeal for the salvation of souls; imitation of the life of our Lord; compassion, admiration, joy; the fear of God's displeasure, of judgment, and of hell; hatred of sin; confidence in the goodness and mercy of God, and confusion for the sins of our past life.[14]

De Sales suggests several books which may be helpful in expanding such affections, but he cautions the reader, whom he calls Philothea, not to "dwell upon these general reflections, without determining to reduce them to special and particular resolutions."[15] He informs Philothea:

The first word our Lord spoke on the cross will doubtless excite in your soul a desire to pardon and love your enemies. But this will avail you little if you add not to the desire a practical resolution, saying: Well, then, I will not hereafter be offended at what this or that person may say of me, nor resent any affront he may offer me; but, on the contrary, I will embrace every opportunity to gain his affection, and to appease him. By this means, Philothea, you will correct your faults in a short time; whereas, by affections only, your amendment will be but slow, and attended with great difficulty.[16]

Resolutions, according to de Sales, are "the great fruit of meditation, without which [meditation] is not only unprofitable, but frequently hurtful. . . . "[17] Resolutions transform grandiose moral aims, such as the desire to love one's enemies, into specific, even mundane, moral tasks, such as being agreeable to a neighbor. The formulation of resolutions is a key step in the process of discursive mental prayer, as taught by de Sales, a step which is designed to transform religious enthusiasm into personal spiritual reform and moral action.

In contrast to de Sales, who accentuates the role of the will in the acquisition of virtue, Liguori highlights the action of God's grace.[18] For Liguori, as in many of the devotions in the prayer books, the acquisition and preservation of grace is central to the spiritual life. This has implications for his understanding of the role of emotion in meditation and the spiritual life more generally.

The method of meditation taught by Liguori is a simplified form of the Salesian method[19] with one major difference; Liguori inserts "petitions" into the body of the meditation between the "affections" and "resolutions."[20] He states:

> In mental prayer it is very profitable, and perhaps *more useful than any other act*, to repeat petitions to God, asking, with humility and confidence, [for] his graces; that is, his light, resignation, perseverance, and the like; but, above all, the gift of his holy love.[21]

These "graces" are the "chief fruit" of meditation, according to Liguori:

> Chiefly for this reason . . . mental prayer is morally necessary for the soul. . . . For if a person does not remember in the time of meditation to ask for [these graces] . . . , he will not do so at any other time; for without meditation he will not think of asking for [them].[22]

According to Liguori, however, these "graces" did not come directly from God; they were mediated through Jesus, Mary, and the saints. Jesus, Mary, and the saints accumulated merits while on earth, which, according to Liguori, they were able to dispense to petitioners. Since the grace they merited came originally from God, they became, in effect, conduits or mediators of grace from God to the petitioner.

The emphasis on the acquisition and the preservation of grace, coupled with the belief in its mediated character, paved the way for a vastly increased emphasis on intercessory prayer to Mary and the saints. Liguori, who is famous for his devotion to Mary, addresses her as "the Mother of my Lord, the Queen of the World, the advocate, the hope, the refuge of sinners." She is his patron, who lavishes graces upon him and rescues him from hell, and upon whom he depends for a "good death."[23] This increased emphasis on intercessory prayer was not limited to meditation; Hail Marys, novenas, the rosary, visits to the Blessed Sacrament and to the Blessed Virgin, scapulars, and confraternities were also promoted by Liguori as effective a means of acquiring and preserving graces.

Many of the specific means of avoiding sin and acquiring graces promoted by Liguori and the Redemptorists were simplified meditations on the passion. Liguori's instructions for the performance of devotions, such as the way of the cross, the rosary, and visits to the Blessed Virgin and the Blessed Sacrament, were all designed to promote meditation on the passion.

The instructions in *The Mission Book* for the way of the cross, for example, explain that "anyone who is in a state of grace may obtain indulgences by making the round of the fourteen stations, meditating before each one upon the mystery it represents."[24] The instructions for the devotion, taken from Liguori, include a description of the mystery, an opening versicle and response, a sentence-length topic for meditation, and a petition. Each meditation relates an event in Jesus' passion to the spiritual life of the devotee. Thus, for example, the meditation for the first station is to "consider how Pilate condemned the innocent Jesus to death, and how thy Redeemer submitted to this sentence, to free thee from the sentence of everlasting death."[25]

In its remarks on the rosary, *The Mission Book* emphasizes that the rosary, if practiced properly, combines both meditation and vocal prayer:

> The meditation is made by the consideration of the most memorable and touching "mysteries" or events in the life, passion, and victory of Jesus Christ our Redeemer. . . . The Mysteries to be meditated on are fifteen in number, and divided into three parts, which are named the five joyful, the five sorrowful, and the five glorious mysteries.[26]

The method of saying the rosary that follows was taken from Liguori and suggests specific topics for meditation in conjunction with each mystery.[27]

Although it was possible to perform such meditations anywhere, the best place for making meditation, according to Liguori, was the church. Jesus, he says, "especially delights in the meditation that is made before the Blessed Sacrament."[28] In his *Visits to the Blessed Sacrament and to the Blessed Virgin*, Liguori gives many "examples of the tender affection with which souls inflamed with the love of God loved to dwell in the presence of the Most Holy Sacrament."[29]

In contrast to de Sales, who viewed Jesus' death as an exemplary act,[30] Liguori viewed it as first and foremost an act of love. "God," according to Liguori, "knew that man is won by kindness" and so determined to "take captive the affections of his heart" by "lavish[ing] his gifts upon him."[31] Meditation on the passion, according to Liguori, awakens the believer to an awareness of sin and to sentiments of love. Liguori emphasizes the details of the passion as a means of arousing the emotions:

> Jesus Christ has suffered so many different pains – the scourging, the crowning with thorns, the crucifixion, etc. – that, having before our eyes so many painful mysteries, we might have a variety of different subjects for meditating on the Passion, by which we might excite sentiments of gratitude and love.[32]

While meditation excites sentiments of gratitude and love, it also awakens the soul to its own sinfulness and its need for assistance in order to love God fully. It is this need for assistance that leads the individual to pray for grace.

This movement from the desire to love God to prayer for the grace to love God fully lies at the heart of meditation for Liguori. Liguori does not eliminate the final step of making resolutions, but they are no longer as central to meditation as they are for de Sales. Liguori channels the believer's desire to love God into fervent petitions rather than directly into specific resolutions for spiritual change and moral action. Thus, he gives freer reign to the emotions and increases the believer's dependence on grace, as opposed to the will.

The freer reign which Liguori gave to the emotions and the increased emphasis which he placed on intercessory prayer as means of acquiring "graces" enhanced the place of devotions in the spiritual life. Through devotions, such as the rosary, the way of the cross, and visits to the Blessed Virgin and the Blessed Sacrament, Liguori made meditations on the passion simpler and more vivid. By promoting devotions which dwelt in greater detail on different aspects of Jesus' suffering, Liguori aimed to "inflame the heart" of the believer with the love of God and contrition for sin. In so doing, he intended to awaken a desire or need in the devotee for supernatural assistance in gaining graces and acquiring virtues. Thus, vivid meditations gave way, at least in theory, to intercessory prayers to powerful intermediaries such as Jesus, Mary, and the saints for the "graces" necessary to bring the will of the believer into conformity with the will of God and thus to grow in perfection.

Unlike Liguori and de Sales, Faber does not promote his own method of meditation. Instead he describes two methods, the Jesuit and Sulpician. The first, like de Sales, emphasizes resolutions; the second, like Liguori, emphasizes petition.[33] Faber's indifference when it comes to method stems, I think, from his belief that the emotions aroused through meditation will inevitably give rise to moral action. It is this confidence that allows him to devote most of his attention to the subject matter of meditation and the generation of affections.

Faber argues that when interior dispositions are put first, the rest is easy. Religion ceases to be a burden, a matter of "weighing commandments, clipping precepts, interpreting rules, [and] begging dispensations" and becomes "a religion of love."[34]

[Jesus expects] from us a rational conviction that our only trust is in Him, and that we should consequently discharge our duties to Him and obey His commandments as our necessary and reasonable service. But He wants far more than this. He has something much nearer His heart. He desires our tenderness. . . . He would fain win us to Himself, and unite us with Himself in the bonds of the most familiar and intimate affection. He would have us identify our interests with His, and concentrate our sympathies in Him. The thought of Him should fill our eyes with tears, and kindle our hearts with love.[35]

According to Faber, "tenderness of its own nature *specializes*. . . . It singles out an object and magnifies it, and for a time excludes other objects from its loving attention."[36] It is this tendency to specialize that generates "special devotions." The ten-

dency to specialize is, for Faber, the key to vividness, and vividness, the key to arousing the affections.

> When . . . we look upon [the passion] as the single mystery . . . it
> is too large for us, and becomes vague. . . . Now, vagueness is pre-
> cisely what we must try to avoid in devotion to the Passion. Its
> virtue resides in its vividness. Unless it be vivid, it will not be
> true; and unless it be true, it will not be reverent. Thus we have
> various devices by which we make the Passion into one mystery
> and yet preserve its details. We take the five trials of our Lord, or
> the seven journeys, or the seven words, or the five wounds. All
> these are excellent contrivances of love.[37]

He says that Jesus' earthly existence may be likened to "a galaxy
of tender mysteries [which] involves special devotions in its very
idea. . . . The gift of piety is the telescope by which we resolve
this galaxy into clusters of constellations or into single stars."[38]
   Thus devotions such as "the Infancy and Passion of our Lord,
the Blessed Eucharist, the dolors of our Lady, [and] the acts
of the martyrs are things especially calculated to win and soften"
—that is, to evoke tenderness. Tenderness, according to Faber,

> was the character our Lord intended to give to His religion; and
> He made every circumstance of the Incarnation and every feature
> of the Church contribute to this unexampled and celestial pathos.
> Every such mystery, circumstance, and feature [thus] becomes in
> its degree the object of special devotion.[39]

In Faber's writings, the devotional proliferation noted in
Liguori's works is even more pronounced. The key to this proliferation, particularly in Faber's case, but also to a certain extent in Liguori's, was pastoral. In the preface to *All For Jesus,*
Faber acknowledges that he was

> not trying to guide souls in high spirituality. . . . God forbid I
> should be so foolish or so vain! As a son of St. Philip [Neri] I have
> especially to do with the world, and with people living in the world
> and trying to be good there, and to sanctify themselves in ordinary
> vocations. It is to such I speak; and I am putting before them, not
> high things, but things which are at once attractive as devotions,

and also tend to raise their fervour, to quicken their love, and to increase their sensible sweetness in practical religion and its duties. I want to make piety bright and happy to those who need such helps, as I do myself.[40]

Faber believed that more affective forms of spirituality were valuable if they allowed the church to reach those who otherwise would not be reached:

> Many are lost, because they are forced too high, and many more, because they are made to fear sensible devotion, and to believe that dryness is solidity. . . . Souls are gravely warned, without regard to time, or place, or person, or condition, to be detached from the gifts of God, and to eschew sweet feelings, and gushing fervours, when the danger is rather in their attachment to their carriages and horses, their carpets and their old china, the parks and the opera, and the dear bright world. Why, if the poor Belgravians could get a little attachment, were it only to an image or a holy water-stoup, and I care not how inordinate, it would be a welcome miracle of grace, considering all they have to keep them far from God, for they move in a sphere which seems to lie outside His omnipresence. No! no! the warnings of St. Theresa to the Barefooted Carmelites are hardly fit for such as those.[41]

While de Sales, Liguori, and Faber all assumed that meditations would arouse the emotions, de Sales's goal was to channel them into specific resolutions for action. The emotional restraint which characterized de Sales's *Introduction* was undermined by Liguori's search for ever more effective ways to "inflame the heart" and by his emphasis on petition in meditation. By channeling emotion into prayer, rather than into resolutions for action, Liguori attempted to unleash the emotions and establish a strong affective bond between the devotee and his or her supernatural patron. Faber's emphasis on affective as opposed to effective love, especially in the beginning stages of the spiritual life, and his confidence that affective love would naturally give rise to effective love, had a similar effect. Liguori and Faber thus both de-emphasized the *methodical* cultivation of virtue which was so prominent in Francis de Sales's *Introduction*, while encouraging the formation of emotionally-charged relationships between the believer and Jesus, Mary, and the saints.

NATURAL AND SUPERNATURAL PARENTS

In his study of Burmese supernaturalism, Melford Spiro provides a psychological explanation of the affective bond between the devotee and the supernatural being which sheds light on the psycho-social dimension of Catholic supernaturalism. To summarize, Spiro suggests:

> Beginning from birth—prior to their acquisition of the *culturally constituted* conceptions of the world made possible by language—children develop *socially constituted* conceptions of the world on the basis of their social experiences with parents and the "significant others" comprising their behavioral environment. Hence, inasmuch as infants are entirely helpless and absolutely dependent on these parenting figures, they construct mental images of incredibly powerful beings long before they learn about the existence of the supernatural beings postulated by their culture. . . . The infant's mental images of his parenting figures are often reified and experienced either as autonomous agents existing in the inner world (whence they are labeled, in the terminology of psychoanalysis, as "introjects") or, since the infant's inner and outer boundaries are blurred, as externalized agents (projections) in the outer world.[42]

When children are then taught about the supernatural beings which inhabit the religious cosmos, they are likely to merge the cultural images of supernatural beings with their images of parental figures to form, in Spiro's words, "a single representational world."[43]

As a result of this merger, cultural symbols for supernatural beings "have both surface-structure and deep-structure meanings simultaneously":

> At the level of surface structure, these symbols represent the *culturally constituted* conceptions of the supernatural beings portrayed by religion and myth—Jahweh, Allah, the Madonna, Siva, Durga, and so on. This is their conscious meaning. At the level of deep structure, they represent the *socially constituted* conceptions of the

parenting figures of childhood. This is their unconscious meaning. In sum, underlying the cross-cultural diversity in the surface meanings of the symbols of mythico-religious beings, there are important cross-cultural uniformities in their deep-structure meanings: the culturally parochial external symbols constitute symbolic transformations of culturally universal internal symbols.[44]

William Henry, Bishop of Natchez, acknowledged the critical role which mothers played in the development of their children's sense of the supernatural in his "Instructions on Mixed Marriages":

> If the mother is not Catholic, what will ever supply for them those early impressions of Catholic piety which it is the mother's place to give? How can the father, engaged all day in his out-door business, teach his children their prayers, give them their first lessons in Catholic faith, and train them from infancy in Catholic practices, to invoke the sweet names of Jesus and Mary, to make the sign of the cross, to love and fear their Guardian Angels, to cherish their medal, to recite the first lessons of the Catechism, to love and imitate the Infant Jesus at Bethlehem and Nazareth? And without these things, the innocent years of childhood are a blank in the Christian life, which after-piety may atone for, but it never can supply, but which more probably will make it impossible for any structure of piety to be built where the foundations have been so neglected.[45]

If, to use Spiro's language, the cultural images of supernatural beings did not merge with the idealized images of parental figures during childhood, it would be very difficult to sustain a deep-seated faith in the supernatural world as an adult.

As we have seen, the affective piety promoted at mid-century made extensive use of parental and familial metaphors. In many instances, images of the natural and supernatural parent were blurred. The apparition of Mary to Archbishop Spalding, described in chapter 3, is a case in point. In that account Spalding uses vivid maternal imagery to refer to the Virgin Mary. However, apart from the linked reference to "My Blessed Mother" and "her Divine Son," the passage could be interpreted as a particularly intense memory or vision of his natural mother. Indeed, his nephew suggests that there were strong, albeit perhaps not conscious, connections between Spalding's memory of his mother and his experience of Mary. According to his nephew, the archbishop told him that "he had lost his own mother . . . when he was five years old, and he had then taken the Blessed Virgin for his mother, and she had had care of him through life." Moreover, the archbishop "several times spoke of his [natural] mother during his last illness, of whose size, features, and gentle ways he said he had a very distinct remembrance, though she had died when he was so young."[46]

In another example, the Rev. Charles Pise, an American priest, associates the recitation of the "Hail Mary" with his earliest memory of his natural mother:

> 'Ave Maria' when in infancy
> I prattled on my gentle mother's knee,
>   She sang that sweet refrain:
> And while all other memories of that day
> Have vanished one by one, like dreams, away—
>   Not so that sacred strain.[47]

A similar association of Mary with both a mother and a wife is made in a European story translated for Ave Maria. In it, the faith of a medieval knight was described as follows:

> The image of our Blessed Lady was to him the symbol of all his faith. He desired Heaven because it was blessed with her sweet presence. . . . He loved to recommend himself to her . . . [and] Mary had never been deaf to his prayers. When any one mentioned Her name, his usual sternness gave way to a more tender air. He would have joyfully shed every drop of his blood for Her, and perhaps it was because he recognized Her form under that of Etiennette, that he submitted so completely to the dominion of his wife. These two affections, the only ones rooted in his heart *since the death of his mother*, had taken entire possession of the bosom of Berenger, no other creature had discovered the way to inspire him with attachment.[48]

These passages suggest that for some Catholics at least there was a strong connection between their attachment to supernatural figures and their often unconscious attachment to their natural parents. Moreover, the fact that such passages often focused on men's relationships with Mary should alert us to the possibility of gender-related differences in establishing or maintaining such attachments.

Many of the mid-nineteenth-century accounts of lapsed Catholics' return to the faith portray affect-laden memories of the mother-child relationship as the vehicle which precipitated their return. Again, it should be noted that the accounts most commonly described *male* Catholics' return to the faith. In one account, it was reported that such childhood memories returned to an old man on his deathbed:

> And then, instantaneously from the depths of his soul, across his darkened mind, and from far away in his early childhood—across seventy-four years—across all those wars and all those battlefields which had passed over his life and effaced from his soul all ideas of religion, came back to this old soldier the remembrance of his mother, and the prayers [the Hail Mary and Our Father] she had taught him when he was a little boy.[49]

In another story, it is the sight of the host carried in a procession that triggered the memory of childhood religion:

> How can I describe the emotion that seized upon me at this sight [of the host]—at the sight of the Saviour, whom I had so long neglected—forgotten—so unworthily forgotten! It was Jesus, going to console and strengthen some dying Christian; Jesus, the first name I had learned in my mother's arms; Jesus, whom I had so often called upon in sinless infancy.[50]

In a final, slightly more complex, example, a young man recalled his dying mother's parting prayer that she might see her child again in heaven and "the remembrance of these words, thus unexpectedly revived in his mind, almost drew tears from his eyes." Later his "unsubdued pride" filling him with "ill-humor,"

> [he] called to account his own mother, and was tempted to throw her likeness overboard, but at this thought he immediately recoiled, and shuddered with dismay. Turning then his indignation against himself . . . he burst into tears, and found himself, he knew not how, on his knees, bending over his berth, and with his head buried in his hands, imploring amidst his sobs, pardon of his mother, and mercy of God.[51]

As a sign of his conversion, he placed a miraculous medal along with the picture of his mother on a chain around his neck.[52]

In general terms, Spiro's theoretical model thus suggests that human relationships with supernatural beings are constituted from the same psychological stuff as the earliest parent-child relationships. In many of the Catholic examples cited, it is prayer (talking *with* supernatural beings) as opposed to doctrine (talking *about* supernatural beings) which is associated with the parent-child, and particularly the mother-child, relationship. It is in just such a context ("prattl[ing the Ave Maria] on my gentle mother's knee") that we would expect a merger of parental and cultural images to have occurred.

In return for obedience and devotion, supernatural patrons provided the graces and favors believed necessary for salvation or well-being in this world. Insofar as Catholics believed that supernatural beings provided the only means of obtaining what they needed, devotees entered into a dependent relationship with their supernatural patrons. The promotion of such relationships by the clergy played upon their earliest, often unconscious, feelings of dependence on their parents. Thus, just as a small child depends on seemingly godlike parents for survival in this world, so devotions fostered relationships in which childlike humans were dependent on a parentlike god for their survival in the next.

The fact that culturally the formation of a "masculine" identity has required boys to break the mother-son bond of early childhood, while girls often maintain close mother-daughter ties throughout life, may have made affective relationships more difficult for males to establish and maintain.[53] Although men may have had more difficulty expressing such feelings, and thus "lapsed" more frequently, their feelings, when expressed, may have been particularly intense. Such at least appears to have been the case in the accounts already cited. In the first account, a soldier who epitomized "manly" independence, recalled the prayers to his supernatural parents which his mother had taught him. In the second, a man recognized the host as Jesus, the one whom his mother had taught him to recognize as consoler and strengthener. In the third account, a proud, independent thinker, horrified by his hostile feelings toward his mother (whose dying wish had been that they might be supernaturally reunited in heaven) chastises himself for his anger and pride, and reestablishes the bond between himself and his mother/Mary. In this latter case, devotion to Mary is used by the young man as a means of maintaining an idealized image of his mother. By turning his anger at his mother against himself and casting himself as a sinner, he is able to preserve the sort of anger-free relationship presumably desired by his mother and, at least in his mind, sanctioned by God.[54] In each of these cases the opposition between emotional attachment and male autonomy is sharp.

Although in the accounts cited above the focus is on the problematic nature of men's relationships with supernatural beings, women do play an essential albeit supporting role. In most cases they are cast as tender, loving mothers for whom devotion comes naturally and spontaneously. Archbishop Spalding had a "distinct remembrance" of the "gentle ways" of his natural mother, even though she had died when he was five years old; Rev. Pise "prattled on his gentle mother's knee" while she sang the "sweet refrain" of the *Ave Maria*; the angry young man's mother had died praying that she would see her son again in heaven.

The disproportionate number of women in devotional organizations, noted in chapter 1, suggests that devotional relationships may have in fact been less problematic for women than they were for men. At a time when women spent most of their lives enmeshed in family relationships, such devotions may have provided a source of solace and a means of repressing resentments about their familial relationships and responsibilities. The relational character of the devotions, their emphasis on obedience and devotion to idealized supernatural patrons, and their tendency to evoke feelings of dependence corresponds closely to the stereotypically "feminine" role which nineteenth-century women were expected to assume in marriage.

Mission preachers and devotion-oriented spiritual writers, such as Liguori and Faber, deliberately set out to establish strong emotional bonds between human clients and supernatural patrons. In constituting such relationships, preachers probably drew upon Catholics' early experiences with their parents, without necessarily being aware of that fact. In suggesting this, I do not mean to imply that nineteenth-century American Catholics were particularly distinctive in this regard. Indeed, similarly affective forms of piety were being popularized among Protestants during the same period. It makes more sense to suggest that preachers, both Catholic and Protestant, were promoting forms of piety intended to appeal to a wide audience during this period in their attempt to attract and maintain a following in a competitive environment.

5

Orthopraxis and Orthodoxy

Church officials promoted devotions in order to bind the laity more closely to the institutional church, both to ensure the church's survival in this world and to ensure the orthodoxy of the laity and thus their survival in the world to come. The promotion of indulgenced devotions enhanced the hierarchy's control over the laity in two ways: first, by centralizing devotional practices in the parish church and standardizing practices throughout the church as a whole, and second, by creating symbolic associations and patronage relationships between supernatural beings, the pope, and the institutional church. In this way, I will suggest, the affective bond between devotees and their supernatural patrons could be mobilized to serve institutional ends.

Although indulgenced devotions were promoted particularly effectively during the nineteenth century, especially during the pontificate of Pius IX, the ultramontane devotionalism of the nineteenth century was in certain respects simply a renewal of a form of piety that had been codified at the Council of Trent some three hundred years earlier. Recent studies of devotional change in eighteenth-century France and sixteenth- and twentieth-century Spain illuminate the underlying ecclesiological implications of the changes in mid-nineteenth-century American devotional practice.

LOCAL AND GENERAL DEVOTIONS

In a historical study of a French diocese (Vence) during the early eighteenth century, Marie-Hélène Froeschlé-Chopard makes a distinction between the "new devotions" which had been introduced after the Council of Trent and the "popular devotions" which had long been practiced in the diocese. The "new devotions," including the rosary and devotions to the Blessed Sacrament, St. Joseph, and the souls in purgatory, were associated with church-based confraternities; the "popular devotions" were centered on cults of saints and their relics, particularly patron, healing, and protective saints, associated both with special altars in the churches and with rural shrines or chapels.[1]

Froeschlé-Chopard defines popular devotion as "the devotion of the non-clerics as opposed to the clergy."[2] Practically speaking, this means that any religious practices which the episcopal visitation records for the diocese suggest were actively opposed or barely tolerated by the clergy are categorized by Froeschlé-Chopard as popular devotion.[3] She argues that there was a logical opposition between the religion of the clergy and the popular religion, such that they represent "two parallel worlds which are entirely ignorant of one another."[4] The religion of the clergy, which she identifies as Tridentine, accented "the role of the priest as mediator who alone can give the sacraments and therefore confer grace." The popular religion, she says, does not overtly contest the religion of the clergy, but "contradicts it in its gestures and rites." Specifically, she suggests that through popular religious practices people were able to interact directly with God without the help of intermediaries.[5]

In a later article describing the iconography of the sacred places within two eighteenth-century French dioceses (Vence and Grasse), Froeschlé-Chopard describes the "ongoing struggle" between the old and new forms of religion as one in which "a 'new religion,' which stressed the persons of the Trinity and the authority of the Church and reduced the traditional saints to the role of intermediaries, endeavored to push aside an older one, in which the power of the saints was uncontested." The new religion stressed personal morality and the role of the priest as intermediary, while the older tradition held forth the possibility that anyone, lay or clergy, "could reach God directly by appealing to the saints." The religion of the "little people" or non-elites was denounced by the clergy and "relegated to the rural chapels, which were henceforth viewed with vague suspicion and distrust."[6]

Despite the logical and to a certain extent spatial distinctions which Froeschlé-Chopard concludes existed between popular and clerical religion, she describes a considerable amount of practical overlap between them. In fact, it appears from her account that almost everyone adopted the new devotions, just, she argues, not in the same way. Only the village elite who joined the new confraternities of the Blessed Sacrament, rosary, and so on, adopted the new devotions in the way the clergy intended *(tels quels, ou apparemment tels quels)*. The simple *(menu)* people appropriated them in a traditional fashion; devotion to Mary continued through the cult of the rosary, while the veneration of a supernatural power like that thought to inhere in relics continued through devotion to the Blessed Sacrament.[7] Thus, she states, "the [new] cults [were] only apparently received, apparently orthodox: they [were] a new popular [religion, embodying] a whole other signification than that which [was] explicitly given by the doctrine."[8]

In an anthropological study of contemporary Catholicism in northern Spain, William Christian also observed two types of devotion existing side by side. The older form was connected to shrines located in specific places, such as mountain peaks, springs, caves, village boundaries, or the borders of cultivated fields, and could be moved only under "certain rigorous ritual conditions." These shrines, according to Christian, marked points of contact with "other worlds," from the supernatural "world" of the saints to the more prosaic "world" of a neighboring village. Both communal and individual devotions were performed at these sites; in both cases, Christian claims devotions were performed in order to "influence the course of crises and ensure the normal unfolding of the life process."[9]

Successive waves of new devotions were brought to the valley during the nineteenth and early twentieth centuries by missionary priests and the better-educated parish priests assigned to the valley from outside. Unlike the older devotions, the new devotions had no connection to the land; they were generalized or universal. The missionaries and some of the priests used these new devotions in their "struggle to ethicalize the religion, to change it from an instrumental set of outward observances into a deepened, more inward spiritual life."[10]

The generalized devotions, which were designed as aids to salvation, belonged to the post-Tridentine period, while the local devotions, which served instrumental ends, had pre-Tridentine roots. According to Christian, these two logically and historically distinct modes of devotion interpenetrated and made mutual adjustment. He notes that with few exceptions the local devotions were tolerated by the priests, while some of the people responded to the clerical emphasis on salvation. Moreover, he suggests that the "local devotions" were sometimes used for redemptive purposes, while some of the "generalized devotions," such as scapulars, devotions to the souls in purgatory, and devotion to the Sacred Heart, were "adopted by the people for use as patrons and shrine images" and thus "utilized for practical aims."[11]

Froeschlé-Chopard and Christian both distinguish between devotions introduced before and after the Council of Trent. Both associate devotions introduced prior to Trent primarily, but not exclusively, with extraparochial shrines and chapels, and those introduced after Trent with the parish church. Froeschlé-Chopard simply called the devotions introduced after Trent "new" devotions, while Christian identified them as "general" or "universal" devotions in contrast to older, "local" devotions. Further, despite their efforts to distinguish logically between two forms of devotion – one clerical and the other popular, in Froeschlé-Chopard's case, and one purificatory and the other instrumental, in Christian's case – both acknowledge that a considerable degree of syncretism occurred in practice.

Identification of local devotions with extraparochial shrines and chapels, and general devotions with the parish church, is useful most, but not all, of the time. Thus, for example, nineteenth-century churches could contain altars dedicated to local saints, while local shrines, such as that at Lourdes, could be replicated and thereby generalized. Moreover, those general devotions that were worn on the person or performed at home were church-based only in the attenuated sense that the objects were usually acquired at a church.

These categories begin to cause difficulties only if we assume that there was an essential or logical difference between general and local devotional practices. In a more recent book on local religious practices in sixteenth-century Spain, Christian moves away from this assumption, suggesting that there has been "a two-way relation between local and universal religion" throughout the history of Catholicism. In practice, he argues, new agents have continually introduced new universal devotions in an attempt to create "a commonality across boundaries of place and nation," while local populations have continually "adapt[ed] and coopt[ed] . . . the general agents and devotions for local purposes."[12]

Because both local and generalized devotions could be appropriated in a variety of ways by both clergy and laity, it would be more accurate to define the difference between general and local devotions sociologically rather than substantively. Thus, general devotions were authorized by the pope for promotion in standardized form throughout the church. Because they were standardized, general devotions required both printing and literacy for their dissemination. Local devotions were not approved by the pope for promotion throughout the church and thus were not standardized from one place to the next. Local devotions could be transmitted orally and did not presuppose literacy.

Local devotions per se were not frowned upon by the hierarchy. Although sometimes rejected as superstitious, local devotions were at other times ignored, or sometimes even promoted and approved by the hierarchy in and for a national or regional subgroup within the church. In some cases local devotions were inherently local, in the sense that they could not be moved; in other cases they could have been generalized.

Virtually all general devotions began as local devotions, often receiving papal sanction as general devotions only after vigorous lobbying efforts on their behalf. Although few if any general devotions were invented by the papacy, devotions which had been generalized, by definition, took on meaning for the institutional church as a whole. Virtually all of the devotions in the prayer books and devotional guides published in the United States at mid-century were generalized devotions. They were therefore by definition not exclusively or even particularly American.

Using this sort of definition we would not expect all general devotions necessarily to be parish-related or all local devotions to be shrine- or chapel-related, though most in fact were. The absence of a perfect fit between categories can be accounted for if we postulate two processes underlying the distinctions made by Froeschlé-Chopard and Christian: one, a movement of devotions from extraparochial shrines and chapels into the parish church, and the other, a movement to universalize and thus to standardize particular devotional practices throughout the church. If we presuppose a desire on the part of the hierarchy to enhance its control over the devotional life of the laity, then the overlap between these two processes should not be surprising.

THE CENTRALIZATION AND STANDARDIZATION OF PRACTICE

Efforts to centralize and standardize religious practice emerged in the wake of the Counter-Reformation. According to John Bossy:

> The Church of the last medieval centuries was not in actual fact a parochially-grounded institution. The disciplinary significance of the council of Trent and of two centuries of activity on the part of the Catholic hierarchy [of France and Italy] lay in their determination that it should effectively become so grounded.[13]

Thus, "what the Counter-Reformation really meant [to the laity] was the institution among them, by bishops empowered by the council of Trent to enforce it, of a system of parochial conformity."[14] The centralization and, even more, the standardization of devotional practice were linked to the use of indulgences. Indulgences, however, took on this function only after they lost their revenue-generating potential in the wake of Protestant criticism and Catholic reform.

Pilgrimages to holy places and alms-giving were the most common forms of pious work for which indulgences were originally offered. Plenary indulgences were first granted on a large scale as a means of promoting the crusades and from 1095 to 1300 they were offered almost exclusively for pilgrimages to Jerusalem or to those who aided such pilgrims.[15] With the loss of the Holy Land, indulgences were also granted for pilgrimages to Rome. In 1300, Boniface VIII granted a plenary indulgence to all who made a pilgrimage to Rome, a privilege which by 1500 was routinely granted every twenty-five years.[16]

The idea that "the devotion manifested and the fatigues endured in the pilgrimage entitled [the pilgrims] to a diminution of the inflictions provided in the canons" was soon extended to less important, but more accessible pilgrimage sites.[17] During the late Middle Ages, multitudes of local "shrines desirous of attracting pilgrims and their oblations . . . [sought] to obtain privileges establishing a fixed term of diminution of penance as an equivalent for a visit to them accompanied by a donation."[18] Many shrines were in fact indulgenced both by the popes and by local bishops.[19]

As the Counter-Reformation church abandoned indulgences as a means of generating revenues, "it became more and more liberal in its use of them for the purpose of stimulating acts of devotion and enabling the religious Orders [who conducted parish missions] to extend their influence."[20] Beginning in the sixteenth century, a new type of indulgence was issued which was attached to *objects*, such as rosaries, crosses, crucifixes, statues, and medals, rather than to *places*.[21] To gain the indulgence the owner of the blessed object was not required to make a pilgrimage. Rather, according to *The Raccolta*, the owner was required to visit a church or public oratory, go to confession and communion, and perform specified devotional acts or recite specified prayers.[22] In addition to the prayers for the specific

devotion, Catholics were often instructed to pray "for the intention of the Sovereign Pontiff" or "for the usual intentions,
[i.e.,] . . . for the spread of the Catholic faith, for the triumph
of the holy Church, for the conversion of sinners, for peace and
union among Christian princes and rulers, and for the extirpa-
tion of heresy." The form of these prayers was left up to the
believer.[23]

Thus the apostolic indulgences were general in that they did
not require travel to a particular place; they could be acquired
anywhere that a priest and a church were available. Such indulgences dramatically increased the clergy's control over the
religious life of the laity by requiring confession and communion, by focusing devotional life on the parish church, and by
standardizing the devotions practiced and prayers recited.

Partly in response to changes in indulgences, confraternities
also shifted their devotional focus from shrines and chapels to
the parish church. Medieval confraternities were voluntary associations with members from a common geographical area or
profession. They maintained a salaried clergy and often had independent chapels or associations with particular shrines.[24]

According to Bossy, attempts were made to bring confraternities under more direct episcopal control during the sixteenth
century.[25] These efforts were facilitated by the post-Tridentine
decrees of Clement VIII and Paul V, which prohibited the granting of indulgences in return for entrance fees while dispensing
them liberally in return for approved acts of devotion.[26]

There is considerable evidence that attempts to regulate the
confraternities proceeded slowly. In a study of clergy-lay relations in the eighteenth-century French diocese of Dauphiné,
Timothy Tackett found that both types of confraternities were
still present. Of the two most widespread confraternities in the
diocese—confraternities of the rosary and of penitents—one was
of each type. In Dauphiné, according to Tackett, the post-
Tridentine confraternities of the rosary were primarily organizations for women. Most of the rosary confraternities' activities
were devotional. According to Tackett, the women were expected
to attend special prayer sessions for the Virgin at various times

during the year and to recite the rosary in unison before a special altar in the church. In return, members were able to gain special indulgences granted by the pope.[27]

Unlike the rosary confraternities which existed in many parts of Europe, the penitents' confraternities were limited to southern France and the Mediterranean region. Also in contrast to the rosary confraternities, most of the members of the penitents' confraternities were men, some of them quite prominent in their local communities. According to Tackett, the aim of the penitents' confraternities was "to do penance for the transgressions . . . against God, and thus to obtain special indulgences for Purgatory."[28] The penitents' confraternities also performed a variety of functions at funerals, taking on in effect, "the function of a village burial society."[29]

Unlike the rosary confraternities, each confraternity of penitents maintained a chapel which was "usually quite distinct from the parish church, whether in the tribune at one end of the church or in an entirely separate building elsewhere in the village." Some of the penitents' groups even had their own chaplains.[30] While the rosary confraternities were strongly supported and closely supervised by the parish priests, the penitents' confraternities were "a source of considerable difficulty for a curé" to quote one of the local priests.[31] Their most galling offense, according to Tackett, was that they "seemed to be establishing a kind of parallel cult, separate from and in competition with the regular parish mass."[32]

Although there is disagreement as to when and if these more autonomous types of confraternities died out,[33] it is certain that clerically controlled parish-based confraternities were revitalized on the continent and established for the first time on a large scale in England, Ireland, and the United States during the middle decades of the nineteenth century.[34] Although much of the impetus for founding such organizations originally came from the religious orders that conducted parish missions, Pius IX facilitated their organization in 1861 with a decree confirming the bishops' practice of appointing parish priests as rectors of the organizations and empowering priests to bless the scapulars, chaplets, and other objects which conferred indulgences on the members.[35] It was at the next Plenary Council of Baltimore in 1866 that the American bishops, now formally in control of the societies within their respective dioceses, went on record as favoring the establishment of such organizations.[36]

These clerically controlled parish-based organizations provided a model for a somewhat more modern type of confraternity which made use of the periodical press to create national and even international networks of confraternities.[37] In the United States, there were, as we saw in chapter 3, at least three nationally organized confraternities of this type: the Archconfraternity of Our Lady of the Immaculate Conception and the Association of Our Lady of the Sacred Heart, both associated with *Ave Maria*, and the Apostolate of Prayer, associated with the *Messenger of the Sacred Heart*.[38] All three were founded in France during the nineteenth century and received the papal sanctions necessary to affiliate groups on an international basis. Though international in scope, the organizations each had a national headquarters and a national periodical.

Despite the Tridentine emphasis on centralization, the nineteenth-century church, largely for pastoral reasons, took a more positive attitude toward the thaumaturgical devotions traditionally associated with holy places, and attempted to incorporate them into officially approved practices in ways which would not compromise the hierarchy's control.[39] Although these new confraternities were not founded to promote miraculous cures, the thaumaturgic element which usually developed in response to lay pressure soon came to be an important attraction.[40] These organizations were thus able to combine the thaumaturgic possibilities of a shrine with the clerical control of a parish-based organization, while at the same time eliminating the need for costly pilgrimages.

Some pilgrimage sites were established in the United States at mid-century. Ralph and Henry Woods's *Pilgrim Places in North America* lists eleven shrines established in the United States prior to 1880.[41] Five of the shrines were established by importing relics or a replica of a sacred image, such as a statue or a painting of Mary, from Europe or by replicating a holy place, such as Lourdes, in its entirety. Six of the shrines were founded in response to an alleged supernatural event which occurred in this country. Three involved acts of protection (from a plague, from defeat by the British at the Battle of New Orleans, and from death after an accident), one a miraculous cure, and one a vision. In a final case, a church dedicated to the Immaculate Conception and located on top of Mount Adams, the highest point in the Cincinnati area, became a pilgrimage spot as soon as construction began. Why Archbishop Purcell authorized a church on Mount Adams is not explained, but it is possible that, as the highest point around, it was perceived as a sacred place in its own right.

Most of the shrines were founded by clergy or religious from France or Germany. The only shrine founded by a lay person was the Chapel Shrine of the Immaculate Conception (the "Wisconsin Lourdes") in Robinsonville, Wisconsin. The shrine was established in response to the visions of Adele Brice, a young lay woman to whom Mary appeared as the Immaculate Conception. Three of the shrines were associated with convents. Most of the rest were associated with churches, mainly churches run by religious orders. Almost all of the shrines reported cures of pilgrims through the intercession of their patron, though few if any were officially recognized.

Pius IX encouraged the replication of the shrine at Lourdes and approved the sale of bottled Lourdes water, which Americans could order through *Ave Maria*. He also blessed and granted indulgences for pilgrimages to replicas of the basilica of Our Lady of the Angels near Niagara Falls and at Notre Dame, Indiana, and a replica of the Holy House of Nazareth at St. Mary's near Notre Dame, Indiana; pilgrims to any of these shrines received the same indulgences as those who visited the French or Italian originals.[42]

The devotion to the *Mater admirabilis*, or the fifteen-year-old Mary Immaculate, although fairly obscure, provides a good illustration of the process by which a shrine could be generalized. The devotion originated with a fresco of the fifteen-

year-old Mary on a convent wall in Rome. The fresco was not
particularly remarkable as a work of art, but "since the year 1846,
when the Holy Father gave his solemn blessing to the picture,
remarking that 'it was a pious thought to represent the most
Holy Virgin at an age when she seemed to have been forgotten,'
signal favors have repeatedly been bestowed upon persons who
have prayed before it." Among them were a "great number" of
miraculous cures and "multitudes of sinners who came out of
mere curiosity to gaze upon [the] picture . . . were converted by
an instantaneous infusion of divine grace."[43]

> In 1849 Pope Pius IX., by an apostolic brief, granted permission
> for the celebration of the festival of the *Mater admirabilis* on the
> 20th of October, and enriched the sanctuary with indulgences. In
> 1854, by a second rescript, he confirmed an indulgence of three
> hundred days, which he had previously granted verbally to all the
> faithful who should recite three Hail Marys before this holy paint-
> ing, adding the invocation, *Mater admirabilis, ora pro nobis*; and
> in the following year the indulgences were extended to the entire
> order of the Sacred Heart. The devotion to the "Mother most ad-
> mirable" spread rapidly, and copies of the painting at the *Trinità*
> were soon to be found in various parts of Europe and America.[44]

A reproduction of the painting, along with accounts of "conversions, vocations, and cures" and devotional writings by pu-
pils at the Roman convent, were then arranged by Father Monnin as a book of devotions for the month of May.[45] Shrines and
the practices associated with them thus were tolerated and sometimes even encouraged by Pius IX and the American hierarchy
as long as they were supervised by the clergy or religious.

Of the shrines founded in the United States at mid-century
only one, the Chapel Shrine of the Immaculate Conception in
Robinsonville, Wisconsin, met with ecclesiastical opposition.
According to the Woodses, an apparition of Mary calling herself the Queen of Heaven appeared to Adele Brice and told her
to "devote her life to bringing [the settlers and their children]
back to their faith." According to the Woodses' account, this call
transformed her from "a shy, unlettered, diffident country girl"

into a speaker of "fiery eloquence and fervor." Although the Woodses are careful not to refer to her as a preacher, she traveled from village to village, "spreading word of her mission, teaching children the rudiments of their faith . . . and exhorting their parents to return to the Church." Her activities apparently drew large crowds, "won many converts," and led other young women to join her. Brice's father built a small chapel shrine in honor of the apparition on land donated by a neighbor for that purpose.

Brice's activities aroused the opposition of the local clergy, who "characterized her visions as myths" and threatened her with excommunication. The account states that she and her followers "eventually . . . were admitted as postulants into the Third Order of St. Francis." The shrine "became a favored spot for those who sought the intercession of Our Lady, and many miraculous cures of the lame, the blind and the sick are attributed to the help of the patroness of the little wayside shrine."[46]

Several points stand out in the brief account given by the Woodses. First, Brice was not only teaching children, she was also "exhorting their parents [with] . . . fiery eloquence and fervor." She was preaching, winning converts, and attracting followers. Nineteenth-century women *religious* were not allowed to preach; Brice was a lay woman, who only belatedly joined an order. Second, Brice claimed to have been told to do these things by Mary herself. The clergy challenged the authenticity of a vision which granted a lay woman the authority to preach, and threatened to excommunicate her. Although the local authorities opposed her, she was apparently not excommunicated. Third, a shrine commemorating the Virgin's appearance was built by Brice's father, on land donated by a neighbor. Though established by lay people rather than clergy or religious, activity at the shrine itself seems to have been similar to that at most other shrines. Brice and her followers eventually joined the Third Order of St. Francis and although Brice managed the shrine until her death, her order seems to have been officially in charge of the chapel.

Reading between the lines, we may infer that it was Adele

Brice's eventual willingness to bring herself, her followers, and her shrine under the supervision of a religious order that prevented her excommunication.

DEVOTIONS AND AUTHORITY

Both Froeschlé-Chopard and Christian suggest that the major difference between post-Tridentine and earlier forms of Catholicism lay in the way that people gained access to the supernatural. Under the older system, the individual had direct access, they argue, to graces and favors through divine intermediaries, while under the new system all graces and favors were mediated through the clergy.[47] The contrast, at least in the nineteenth-century American context, was not this sharp. Rather than eliminating the possibility of obtaining graces and favors through divine intermediaries, the emphasis on the priest and the sacraments simply attempted to subordinate practices associated with relics, saints, and shrines to practices such as confession and communion. The distinction between sacrament and sacramental, i.e., those approved practices which were not sacraments, which emerged during the medieval period and was codified at Trent, was one of reliability, not efficacy. Miracles were irregular or unpredictable manifestations of grace worked by God to honor the saint petitioned.[48] Thus, although the priest controlled the only means of remitting mortal sins (confession) and the most reliable means of receiving graces and favors (communion), graces and favors could also be granted directly by God to the laity through supernatural intermediaries.

Thus, relative to the older, pre-Tridentine forms of devotion, ultramontane devotionalism not only centralized and standardized practice, but also subordinated devotions to Mary and the saints to devotion to Jesus in the Blessed Sacrament. Saints were played down relative to Jesus and Mary; Mary was subordinated, at least in theory, to Jesus; and sacramentals were subordinated, again at least in theory, to the sacraments. Although graces and favors could be obtained from Mary and the saints by means of general devotions just as they had been obtained from pilgrimages to holy places, official teachings emphasized that Mary and the saints were merely mediators of graces and favors obtained through Jesus' sacrificial death. All graces and favors radiated outward or downward from Jesus to Mary, the saints, and the faithful at large.

The Catholic understanding of the Mass as the unbloody repetition of Jesus' sacrificial death on Calvary and hence of Jesus' real presence in the wafer was the linchpin connecting the supernatural hierarchy (of Jesus, Mary, the saints, and the faithful) to the earthly hierarchy (of pope, bishop, priest, and laity). For just as supernatural beings were ranked on the basis of their degree of access to supernatural power or grace, so too were human beings. According to Peter Brown, the distinction between the clergy and the laity was "explicitly designated in terms of varying degrees of contact with the supernatural. The priest was superior to the layman because he handled the holy and the layman did not."[49] By defining those rites which the clergy alone could perform as the only regular means of grace, the medieval theologians limited the laity's means of access to the holy, at least in theory, and thus enhanced the power of the clergy.[50] Veneration of the Blessed Sacrament tacitly affirmed this set of presuppositions and thus helped to enhance the distinction between clergy and laity.

Although ultramontane devotionalism did subordinate devotion to Mary and the saints to devotion to Jesus, this probably would have had more significance for theologically unsophisticated Catholics than for well-educated lay Catholics raised on Francis de Sales and *The Garden of the Soul*. From the point of view of the latter, ultramontane devotionalism, by emphasizing intercessory prayer, the sacramentals, and devotion to Mary and the saints at all, expanded and anthropomorphized the realm of the sacred at the expense of the methodical meditations on the passion to which they were accustomed. Thus, from their point of view, the more significant change was probably the growing emphasis on passion meditations performed in the church in the presence of Jesus in the Blessed Sacrament. By shifting the backdrop against which passion meditations were performed, ultramontane devotionalism identified the object of the passion meditations with the consecrated wafer produced through the action of the priest at Mass. Through this identification, passion meditations, including meditations on the Sacred Heart of Jesus, took on ecclesiological overtones and tacitly participated in the affirmation of clerical authority.

These implicit connections between devotion to the Blessed Sacrament and clerical authority were explicitly spelled out by F. W. Faber in a sermon entitled "Devotion to the Pope," which was published in pamphlet form in the United States in 1860 for mass distribution. Faber begins the sermon with the idea that Jesus, the center of the Christian's life, is still present in the Blessed Sacrament. "The thirty-three years are not over," he says. In fact:

> [Jesus] is more accessible to us now than He could have been in the actual Three-and-Thirty Years. . . . We can have Him more completely to ourselves. We can enjoy Him more at ease, and more in private. Hence it is that the Blessed Sacrament is the very centre of our lives.[51]

Yet, Faber goes on to say:

> Our love needs more than this. . . . Our life is very much a life of matter, sense, and outward things. In the Blessed Sacrament Jesus is invisible. . . . The visible Jesus was in some ways sweeter, in some ways dearer.[52]

Jesus, Faber claims, has made up the loss of his visible presence by finding fitting representatives of himself on earth. Although, says Faber, Jesus chose the poor and children as visible representatives of himself, "this was not enough."

> [For] when we serve our dearest Lord in the persons of the Poor and of the Children, we are, as it were, His superiors. . . . He goes before us in pitiable plight, and we are full of pity, and we run to His rescue.[53]

According to Faber, to serve those less well off or weaker than ourselves is not the highest form of love:

There are other kinds of love, to which we reach as we grow in grace. . . . We want to obey. We want to receive commands, to hearken to teaching, to practice submission. . . . We want to give up [our own wills] for the will of Him we love. We want to conquer the selfseeking of our understandings, in order that our hearts may grow larger and we may be able to love more vehemently and more exclusively. We want more immolation of self in our service of Jesus than the tending of the Poor and the Children can supply.[54]

The solution, of course, is devotion to the pope. According to Faber, "the Sovereign Pontiff is a third visible presence of Jesus amongst us. . . . The Pope is the Vicar of Jesus on earth. . . . By divine right he is subject to none. . . . He is a monarch. . . . He is the visible shadow cast by the Invisible Head of the Church in the Blessed Sacrament."[55] Thus, to serve and obey the pope is to serve and obey God, and indeed to conform oneself more fully to the will of God.

Faber's emphasis on the importance of obedience to the will of God is not new, nor is his assumption that to conform oneself to the will of God one must abandon oneself. These themes were found in the writings of de Sales and Liguori, as well as in much of the Christian devotional tradition. What is typically Faberian is the use of a devotion, in this case devotion to the pope, as a means of acquiring a virtue, in this case obedience, and thwarting self-love. Obedience to the pope has become for Faber a means of attaining closer union with God. Moreover, the conflation of Jesus and the pope meant that the dependent, childlike relationships which devotions typically fostered with supernatural beings could also be fostered with the "holy father."

What is particularly interesting about all this is that Faber recognized that Pius IX was not the sovereign monarch he wished him to be. He acknowledges that there are indeed times "when the bark of Peter has seemed to be foundering in the midnight seas." Indeed, he says, "we are fallen upon one of those evil epochs now."[56] The result is that "to the unbelieving eye, the Papacy like most divine things, is a pitiable and abject sight, provoking only an irritated scorn. For this scorn," he says, "it is the object of our devotion to make constant reparation."[57]

That there was a contrast or even a gulf between what the believer saw with the "eye of faith" and what others saw through "unbelieving eyes" would not have been a shock to the devotion-minded Catholic, for the Sacred Heart of Jesus present in the Blessed Sacrament suffered daily from the same ignominious treatment as the pope. Indeed, much devotion to the Sacred Heart involved making reparations to it for the humiliation brought upon it by those who did not believe that Jesus was truly present in the Blessed Sacrament. Thus, to make devotional reparations to the pope for the humiliation he suffered at the hands of those who did not recognize his rightful sovereignty as Vicar of Christ would seem only logical to those already making reparations to the Sacred Heart. Moreover, the two might become indistinguishable if the believer took seriously Faber's claim that Jesus was visibly present in the pope just as he was invisibly present in the Blessed Sacrament.

Devotions, Doctrine, and the Integrity of the Church

"Special devotions" were, as Faber pointed out, "essentially doctrinal devotions" and, in keeping with the uncompromising spirit of late Tridentine or ultramontane Catholicism, they stressed precisely those doctrines which Protestants rejected. Some—such as Blessed Sacrament devotions; devotions to Mary, particularly as the Immaculate Conception; and devotions to the souls in purgatory—embodied exclusively Catholic doctrines. Others, such as passion devotions and devotions to the Sacred Heart, though not exclusively associated with Catholicism, linked the passion and the eucharistic wafer and thus highlighted the Catholic understanding of the Mass as sacrifice.

Moreover, virtually all Catholic devotions, including novenas, scapulars, and devotions to the saints and their relics, presupposed the Catholic understanding of the communion of saints and the spiritual economy of merits and satisfactions. The use of indulgences to promote devotions was simply a higher-level manifestation of the same phenomena. As Faber explained, the desire for indulgences was "almost an infallible sign of a good [ultramontane] Catholic," for "indulgences mix us up with so many peculiarities of the Church, from the jurisdiction of the Holy See to the belief in purgatory, good works, the saints, and satisfaction, that they almost ensure our orthodoxy."[58]

Viewed doctrinally, devotions were an intentionally and aggressively Catholic phenomenon which identified orthodoxy with an affirmation of and indeed an emphasis on that which was distinctively Catholic in the realm of doctrine. Devotions thus set the Catholic and non-Catholic, the orthodox believer and the heretic, apart in a clear and distinctive way. Through its use of the symbolic language of purity and defilement, the doctrine of the Immaculate Conception, defined by Pius IX in 1854, articulated this dualistic outlook both doctrinally and devotionally.[59]

The apostolic constitution which declared that "the most Blessed Virgin Mary, in the first instant of her Conception, . . . was preserved free from all stain of original sin," used a variety of terms to characterize Mary, including innocent, pure, holy, perfect, immaculate, unstained, unblemished, and spotless. Her immaculateness is defined by the absence of stain, blemish, and spot. In these latter concepts, we have an allusion to evil as a substance which defiles. Defilement is, according to Paul Ricoeur, not literally a stain, blemish, or spot; nor, however, is it a moral abstraction. Rather, Ricoeur states, "the representation of defilement dwells in the half-light of a quasi-physical infection that points to a quasi-moral unworthiness."[60] By failing to distinguish between the physical and the ethical in its demarcation of the sacred and the profane, the language of defilement is able to connect the biological fact of conception with the ethical idea of (original) sin.

According to Ricoeur, the idea that sex is defiling is both ancient and widespread, and gives rise to a complementary linkage between virginity and purity. Thus, he states, "virginity and spotlessness are as closely bound together as sexuality and contamination."[61] Carrying this logic to the limit, "the infant would be regarded as born impure, contaminated from the beginning by the paternal seed, by the impurity of the maternal genital region, and by the additional impurity of childbirth." Ricoeur adds:

> It is not certain that such beliefs do not continue to prowl in the consciousness of modern man and that they have not played a decisive role in speculation on original sin. Indeed not only does this notion remain dependent on the general imagery of contact and contagion, which it uses in speaking of the transmission of the primordial taint, but it is still magnetized by the theme of sexual defilement considered as pre-eminently the impure.[62]

Throughout the constitution, Mary is juxtaposed with the serpent, another symbol of evil. The constitution states that "it was fitting that so wonderful a mother should be . . . so completely free from all taint of original sin that she would triumph utterly over the ancient serpent."[63] Or again, "the most holy Virgin, united with [Christ] by a most intimate and indissoluble bond, was, with Him and through Him, eternally at enmity with the evil serpent, and most completely triumphed over him, and thus crushed his head with her immaculate foot."[64] Because, by means of divinely given power, she never "lent an ear to the serpent," Mary "utterly destroyed the force and dominion of the evil one." Eve, who ("while yet a virgin, while yet innocent, while yet incorrupt, while not yet deceived by the deadly snares of the most treacherous serpent") was, like Mary, without original sin, "listened to the serpent . . . [and] fell from original innocence."[65]

Both Mary and Eve were born without original sin. Eve lost her purity/virginity because she listened to evil; Mary "ever increased her original gift" and indeed conquered evil by refusing to listen to it. Purity, the constitution suggests, can be maintained free from contamination and corruption simply by paying no heed to the temptations of evil. That which is "set apart" is pure or holy; contamination occurs through contact, specifically through sexual, social, and intellectual intercourse with evil.

To understand why the doctrine of the Immaculate Conception was defined when it was, we need to remember Mary

Douglas's well-known maxim that "the body is a model that can stand for any bounded system."[66] As an acknowledged "type" of the church, the concern with Mary's inviolability and purity reflected, most specifically, the papacy's concern with the political inviolability of the church in the Italian context. In broader terms, however, it expressed the papacy's need to defend its authority to define truth in the modern world.

The constitution implicitly draws the parallel between Mary and the church when it claims that the Roman church is "the mother and teacher of all churches," just as Mary is the mother and teacher of the faithful. Moreover, "such dignity and authority belong to the church that she alone is the center of truth and of Catholic unity." The Roman church alone possesses this authority because, like Mary, it alone has been "inviolably preserved."[67] It is the doctrinal purity of the Roman church, in other words, which allows it to mediate or bear forth the tradition to all other churches, just as Mary's purity allowed her to bear forth the son of God.

In the words of Gerhard Ebeling:

> Mary, the Mother of Christ, the Bride of Christ, the new Eve, answering to the Adam-Christ typology, is *the mythical personification of the Church*, which sees itself as mediating all the gifts of grace. The Church is that which is prefigured in Christ, in that she is the co-redemptrix of all mankind. The Church is not only that which daily accomplishes the sacrifice of the Mass, but has already offered up the Son of God at Golgotha. The Church is thus the mediatrix of the Mediator. No man can come to Christ save through Mary, that is, through the Roman Catholic Church. Yet all this is not explicitly stated, but is symbolized in Mary, and finds its whole metaphysical reality in the person of the divine Virgin.[68]

Thus, according to Ebeling, "the worship of Mary makes it permissible, without making it obvious, for the church to be transformed from the *place* of worship to the *object* of worship."[69] This conflation of Mary and the church, like the conflation of the Sacred Heart and the pope, allowed the emotions aroused

by devotion to Mary, "mother of the faithful," to attach themselves to the institutional, or "mother," church.

Mary, however, was more than just a model for the church:
she was the church's patron or guardian as well. As a patron
of the church, Mary protected it, just as she protected individuals. According to Faber, "the interests of the Church are in especial manner her interests; and as queen of the apostles she
watches with a particular vigilance over the fortunes of the Holy
See."[70] Because of her purity, Mary provided a refuge from and
protection against the evils which threatened the church. According to the apostolic constitution on the Immaculate Conception, she, "who crushed the poisonous head of the most cruel
serpent . . . is the safest refuge and most trustworthy helper of
all who are in danger . . . [and] the most excellent glory, orna-
ment, and impregnable stronghold of the holy Church."[71]

It was, however, as the one "who conquered and destroyed
all heresies"[72] that Mary manifested a particular concern for the
purity of the church. It was because of her antipathy to heresy
that, according to Faber, "devotion to Mary assumes a very pe-
culiar importance . . . in an uncatholic country." Calling upon
the language of purity and defilement, he states that "the vigor
of our faith allows us to resist the infection of heresy, and to
pass unscathed by the poison of its touch." He calls on Catholics "in the foul air of a Protestant land" to fortify their faith
by observing the Marian feasts, joining confraternities, saying
the rosary, and wearing scapulars.[73]

The Sacred Heart, too, could take on the role of a patron.
During the 1870s, many American dioceses were consecrated
to the Sacred Heart, thus placing both the diocese itself and
its members under the patronage of the Sacred Heart. This action was "peculiarly suited to our present wants," according to
Archbishop James Roosevelt Bayley of Baltimore, because "God
is forgotten [and] . . . men have declared their independence of
[God]." Drawing on the language of purity and defilement,
through the use of the metaphor of contagion, Bayley goes on
to explain that "the hearts of men are hardened against . . . the
influence of religion" and emotions which it inspires. This is

due, he claims to "the deadly poison of materialism and sensuality" which surrounds Catholics on all sides and threatens to infect them. "We need some heavenly antidote to this venom," he says, "something that will warm our hearts toward God, and banish the worldly spirit of pride and sensuality." The antidote, of course, was devotion to the Sacred Heart.[74]

Devotion to the Sacred Heart of Jesus, like devotion to Mary, was to generate emotions which would bind Catholics to God and banish any inclinations to worldliness. According to Bayley, "[Jesus] gives us His Heart as a model on which to mould ours." The model which Catholics are called to imitate is one of "meekness, humility, obedience to all lawful authority, [and] patience under every trial."[75] Although the devotional literature frequently referred to Mary and the Sacred Heart as patrons who would protect the church in indeterminate, though presumably supernatural, ways, it is clear that reverential attitudes toward supernatural beings could be symbolically extended to the institutional church and its leadership. Once the affective bond was extended to a papal or priestly "father" or to the "mother" church, it could be mobilized to serve institutional as well as personal ends.

The devotional practices promoted during the mid-nineteenth century were thus promoted by the hierarchy to standardize practices within the church internationally; to relocate devotional practices in the parish church under the control of the priest; to distinguish Catholics from non-Catholics; and to rally the laity to the church and its hierarchy in the face of perceived dangers from without. In so doing, they directly and indirectly enhanced the hierarchy's control over the laity, while fostering a distinctively Catholic identity with international as opposed to national or ethnic overtones.

6
Devotions in the
American Context

The separatist attitude of the Catholic Church with respect to American culture and the isolation of Catholics, at least in some aspects of their lives, from the "mainstream" of American life increased during the mid-nineteenth century. In an influential essay, Thomas McAvoy suggested that immigration and nativism were responsible for transforming what had been a reasonably well-accepted and accepting Anglo-American Catholic Church into a militant and culturally isolated church dominated by Irish immigrants.

At mid-century, according to McAvoy, nativist hostility joined immigrant intransigence to overshadow the accommodating attitudes of the more "Americanized" Anglo-American Catholics.[1] Although McAvoy refers to the "defeatist attitude" of the Anglo-American Catholics, he concludes the article by stating that the aggressive stance of the immigrant Catholics, though understandable in the face of nativist hostility, was misguided because it cut them off from the dominant culture.[2]

McAvoy's explanation of the growing militance and isolation of the American Catholic Church at mid-century suggests that the most influential factors in its development during this key period were external ones—population movements, immigrant (ethnic) attitudes, and native hostility, rather than internal, specifically Catholic, ones. In this chapter, I will explore the role of internal factors, specifically the rise of devotionalism, in the formation of an English-speaking Catholic subculture in the United States.

The impact of the rise of devotionalism in the American context has generally been overlooked because of a tendency to understand the bishops' legislative attempts to create disciplinary uniformity descriptively, rather than normatively. McAvoy, for example, dismisses the possibility that religious change might have played a role in the formation of the "Catholic minority" with the statement that "by 1829, the date of the first Provincial Council of Baltimore, dogmatic and disciplinary unity had been established in nearly all details."[3] At the same time, relatively recent levels of Irish commitment to the institutional church have been read back into the past and thus attributed to mid-nineteenth-century Irish immigrants to the United States, while other immigrant groups have for the most part been ignored.[4] Only recently have historians begun to look beyond the legislated ideal to the actual practices of the various immigrant groups within the American church in an attempt to describe the interaction between the immigrants and an actively Romanizing hierarchy.[5]

ROMANIZATION AND THE AMERICAN HIERARCHY

According to Derek Holmes:

> The triumph of Ultramontanism was reflected not so much in the definition of papal infallibility as in the transformation of Catholicism within a generation. By establishing a Roman approach to devotion, discipline and theology throughout the Catholic Church, the Roman authorities were able to take over the leadership of the Church, while the first Vatican Council simply defined the structure of the Church in accordance with their understanding of it.[6]

To label the devotions promoted at mid-century as "Roman" is, however, somewhat misleading. As a whole, they were Roman only in that they were authorized and promoted by Rome. Their origins, as we have seen, were in fact varied: some were Italian, some French, and some associated primarily with international religious orders. Once taken up and approved by Rome for use throughout the church, a practice was generalized, and in that sense "Romanized."

Contemporaries were aware that this process was going on. Those who supported it viewed Roman attempts to standardize practices as a means of making the church truly catholic, or universal. Those who opposed it viewed standardization as an imperialistic imposition of particular local customs on the church as a whole. John Lingard, who, along with Charles Butler and others, had been a leader in the movement to accommodate English Catholicism to the thought of the Enlightenment during the early part of the nineteenth century, wrote in 1850:

> There may be need of reform among us on many points I concede: but that reform should be based, not upon *national* customs among the Romans or Italians; but on those among Englishmen. Lights and serenading &c. are to foreigners in Italy the most natural manner of showing respect; not so with us.[7]

The opposing view was articulated by Orestes Brownson in a review of a book by an English Oxford convert. Brownson finds fault with the book because "it is not as bold and energetic as we would wish it, but is far more so than the productions of English Catholics [such as Lingard and Butler] during the last century and the beginning of the present." He goes on to say:

> We have, unhappily, been forced to find fault with nearly all the works that have reached us from the Oxford converts. Mr. Faber is the only one of the converts whose writings we are aware of having seen, whom we have had no occasion to criticise. What we have seen from him is written in a true Catholic spirit, is Catholic to the core. Nevertheless, we have found some noble tendencies in all these converts. They nearly all seem to be free from the common English distrust of the papacy, and if they have any errors, they are not those of the school of Charles Butler. They do not appear to think Catholicity would be improved by being remodelled after the Anglican Establishment, nor are they afraid to say their beads, or ashamed to invoke the saints, and venerate sacred

images and relics. They do not appear to think that Catholicity should be one thing for Englishmen and another for Italians, and they appear to feel that their religion is really *Catholic*.[8]

There is not much evidence of opposition to the Romanization of religious practice on the part of American bishops and priests. Perhaps the most outspoken opposition at mid-century arose from a small group of priests in the New York City area, known in chancery circles as the Accademia.[9] According to James Hennesey, Thomas Becker, a Wilmington priest, arraigned the group on a variety of charges:

> They denigrated devotional practices like saying the rosary, wearing scapulars, venerating relics, and calling on the saints. They would do away with vestments worn by priests celebrating mass and eliminate the use of Latin. They questioned the newly defined dogma of Mary's Immaculate Conception and the church's teaching on her Assumption into heaven. They accused the pope of "absorbing all the members and causing atrophy in the Apostolic College." And of course they would oppose the coming definition of papal infallibility.[10]

Richard Burtsell, whose diary provides us with much of the primary evidence of the inner life of this group, says little to substantiate many of Becker's specific charges. He does make it clear, however, that he was opposed to "Romanizing tendencies" in devotional practice and advocated the use of the vernacular in the celebration of the Mass. Like Lingard, Burtsell objected to "Italian customs such as hand-kissing and foot-kissing etc. being made part of the universal ceremonies of the church: just as Parisian customs would not be made holy, or beautiful if Paris were the center of unity."[11] In a discussion of "French ceremonies," Burtsell also indicated that he thought that "the Romanizing tendencies of French bishops [were] . . . of no great utility."[12] Moreover, his opinion of the Jesuits changed following his seminary days at the Propaganda College at Rome: "Whilst I was in school with the Jesuits, I thought they were the leaders of the age. But now I find them wishing to fossilize us with the habits of the middle ages."[13]

Despite the charge that the group denigrated devotional practices, Burtsell routinely noted devotional activities, such as May devotions, sodality meetings, and the forty hours devotion, which he led in the course of his pastoral work. Moreover, as one who advocated the use of the vernacular in the Mass, he valued the fact that such devotions were, for the most part, in English and thus might be used, despite their standardization, as "a wedge for the change of language in the liturgy."[14]

Most significantly, Burtsell gives the impression that he *valued* cultural and linguistic diversity in the church's ritual life. Like Isaac Hecker, who felt that the "American character" should be taken into account in promoting Catholicism in the United States,[15] Burtsell felt that "the discipline of the church must adapt itself to various ages and countries."[16] Burtsell notes that he and Father Nilan

> agreed on the proposition "that we want a centre of unity in the church for faith & morals alone, [but] not for discipline." This proposition needs many qualifications & modifications: it is the opposite extreme to the centralism now the policy of the church, by which the minutest item of discipline emanates from Rome.[17]

When he refers to the discipline of the church he means the large body of decrees having to do with Catholic religious practice. It was precisely in this area that Burtsell, as he admits, was most radical in his thinking and it was probably this desire for pluralism, rather than uniformity, in religious practice that lay at the heart of Thomas Becker's complaint against the Accademia.

In this, Burtsell was at odds not only with the policy of Rome, but with that of the American hierarchy as well. The latter, although somewhat more independent than their European counterparts in political matters, were according to James Hennesey "substantially as ultramontane as a Manning in England or a Cullen in Ireland."[18] Both Manning and Cullen, it should be noted, played key roles in the Romanization of Catholic life and practice in Great Britain.[19] As Joseph Chinnici has shown, the American bishops paid considerable attention to ecclesiastical discipline at the various nineteenth-century councils and synods. The Second Plenary Council, held in 1866, passed legislation on prayer books, indulgences, parish missions, devotional organizations, and a variety of specific devotions, including benediction of and visits to the Blessed Sacrament, scapulars, litanies, May devotions, and the way of the cross.[20]

In contrast to the cultural pluralism advocated by Catholics such as Richard Burtsell, the American bishops assumed that "every effort [should be made] to see to it that one and the same discipline is every where observed."[21] The American bishops' desire to standardize practice throughout the church as a whole was a reflection of the ultramontane desire to elevate Rome as the center of Catholicism and the pope as arbiter of that which was truly Catholic not only in faith and morals, but also in ritual practice. By promoting generalized devotions, they helped to make their ideal more of a reality.

THE ROMANIZATION OF THE IMMIGRANT IRISH

Although it has often been assumed that the Irish immigrants contributed an innate orthodoxy to the mid-nineteenth-century American church, recent studies have emphasized the discontinuities between prefamine Irish Catholicism and the Romanized forms of devotion adopted by Irish Catholics in Ireland[22] and, I have argued, in the United States at mid-century. These studies usually cite cultural factors, rather than innate dispositions, when attempting to explain the unusually positive response of the Irish (relative to Catholics on the continent) to the Romanizing efforts of the hierarchy in the decades after the famine. Emmet Larkin, William Shannon, and Desmond Fennell all point to identity issues in their explanations.

Shannon, for example, argues that the Irish were able to appropriate Catholicism as a vehicle for national identity in a way that was impossible for many continental Catholics because the Catholic Church in Ireland was not aligned either with the state or the landowning elite. In Ireland, the landowners were Protestant and the church was viewed as an ally of the Irish Catholics in their fight against British colonial rule.[23]

In order to explain the Romanization, as opposed to the Catholicism, of the Irish, Larkin and Fennell point to the growing use of English in Ireland beginning nearly a hundred years before the famine.[24] The decline of Gaelic, hastened by the establishment English-language public elementary schools in Ireland during the first half of the nineteenth century, facilitated the adoption of Romanized practices by the Irish. Larkin and Fennell argue that as the Irish lost the Irish language, they also lost what had been a distinctively Irish form of Catholicism, and that as the differences between Irish Catholics and English-speaking Protestants in Great Britain decreased, the Irish compensated by adopting the aggressive form of Catholicism that the mid-nineteenth-century papacy was promoting.[25] Thus, the "devotional revolution," as Larkin labeled it, both "Romanized" Irish religious practice and, according to Larkin, "provided the Irish with a substitute symbolic language and . . . a new cultural heritage" which protected them from the threat of cultural assimilation by emphasizing their religious distinctiveness.[26] It was, Larkin thus implies, *Roman*, not Irish, Catholicism which formed the basis for Irish national identity.

There is little evidence to suggest that these identity issues disappeared for those who emigrated to the United States. Many of the Anglicized Irish immigrants who wished to assert a distinctive cultural identity in the Protestant-dominated American context found a Romanized form of Catholicism to be an effective vehicle.[27] As Father Thomas H. Burke, an Irish Dominican preacher who lectured extensively in the United States in the 1870s, asserted:

> [You could] take an average Irishman—I don't care where you find him—and you will find that the very first principle in his mind is, "I am not an Englishman, because I am a Catholic!" Take an Irishman wherever he is found, all over the earth, and any casual observer will at once come to the conclusion, "Oh; he is an Irishman, he is a Catholic!" The two go together.[28]

The image of a homogeneous, cohesive subculture in which all Irish were Catholics and all Catholics Irish should not, however, be overdrawn. It was, like the idea of disciplinary uniformity, an ideal advanced by some, rather than a reality. Despite the fact that a Romanized form of Catholicism was an effective carrier of Irish ethnic identity, it was not the only such carrier. According to Dale Light, the Irish nationalist organizations which competed with the church for the loyalty of the immigrant "defined Irish ethnicity in secular terms dependent on Irish descent and an ideological commitment to an Irish national state, while the church labored 'to make Irish, Catholic, and Catholic, Irish.'"[29] According to Thomas Brown, ecclesiastical and nationalist leaders differed sharply in their interpretations of the Irish past:

> For the priest, Irish history was a religious drama, a long martyrdom of a people naturally Christian that was permitted by God in order to spread His Word. Aware of the pleasant irony that the immigrant Irish were carrying Catholicism everywhere throughout the English-speaking world, churchmen saw in that tattered figure an arm of the Lord and in the Famine which sent him forth the mysterious 'logic of God.' Nationalists furiously rejected this fatalism; and argued persuasively that Catholic England had been as destructive of the liberties of the Irish as was Protestant England.[30]

Despite their differences, ecclesiastical and nationalist leaders did not formally disavow each others' commitments. Rather, they maintained a relationship of "uneasy tension," born, Brown implies, of their common dependence on the support of Irish immigrants who for the most part refused to separate their Catholicism and their nationalism.[31]

GENERALIZED DEVOTIONS AND THE PARISH CHURCH

The impact of devotionalism on the life of the parish church can be illustrated by the example of Holy Family parish on Chicago's west side. Founded in 1857 by the Jesuit Arnold Damen,

it soon boasted the largest English-speaking congregation in the
city and one of the largest and most elaborate parish complexes
in the nation.[32] Moreover, several of the church's priests, most
notably Fathers Damen and Cornelius Smarius, were among
the leading mission preachers of the day; they thus spent much
of their time attempting to arouse and institutionalize the type
of piety evident at Holy Family parish in churches run by secular clergy throughout the midwest.[33] As an illustration, Holy
Family church is therefore probably not entirely typical. However, since the parish served as a model for other churches in
its own time, it may be taken to reflect an ideal, whether or not
all parishes were able to live up to it.

According to Brother Thomas Mulkerins, S.J., the parish his-
torian, Father Damen began introducing devotional practices
and founding devotional organizations among his parishioners
shortly after a plain, wooden temporary church building was
erected in 1857. In November of 1857, the first of what were
to become annual novenas in preparation for the Feast of the
Immaculate Conception was celebrated.[34] During the first Lenten
season after the church's establishment, Damen celebrated Mass
daily, "followed by a meditation read to the people, the rosary,
instructions and benediction on Wednesday, and Stations of the
Cross on Friday evening."[35] On the first of May 1858, "the fathers began the beautiful May devotions in honor of Our Lady.
These were held every evening at eight o'clock, and took such
hold upon the people as to mark an increased attendance every
year."[36] In October of 1858, the parish held its first mission week
and beginning a few weeks later, "the devotions to the souls in
Purgatory, during the month of November, were practiced . . .
for the first time in [the] parish."[37]

During the same period, Damen also founded the Archconfraternity of the Immaculate Heart of Mary, the Altar Society,
the Society of St. Vincent de Paul, and the Society of the Holy
Family for Men (later to become the Married Men's Sodality).[38]
At the same time, Damen oversaw an ambitious building pro-
gram. Following the construction of the wooden frame church,
a residence was built for the priests, then a school, and by the

summer of 1860, a permanent Gothic church, built of stone. Despite this feverish building campaign, "Father Damen and his associates," according to Mulkerins, "never lost sight of the spiritual end, which was the motive power of all their actions." Significantly, Mulkerins defines this spiritual end in devotional terms. Specifically, he says that "the [spiritual] end is seen in the regular ministrations and in the various devotions introduced, the novenas, the confraternities, and the sodalities, the courses of lectures and instructions, the Lenten, May and November devotions, the solicitude for the poor, the orphans and the outcast."[39]

Although the exterior of the new Gothic building was not, in Mulkerins's words, "very attractive or prepossessing," the interior of the church, acclaimed by many as "one of the most most beautiful . . . in the United States," embodied the devotional style which had been introduced into the old church.[40]

The church contained three altars, a main altar and two side altars. The main altar stretched the width of the church and extended upward fifty-two feet, to within inches of the ceiling. Nearly everything atop the main altar was designed to foster devotion to the Blessed Sacrament and the passion. Above it was a large Gothic tabernacle with angels on either side in which the consecrated hosts were stored. The "benediction throne" on which the host could be displayed was attached to the "roof" of the lower part of the tabernacle.[41]

The main altar also contained four "cases" of sacred relics. According to Mulkerins, some of these were "very precious, as they contain[ed] fragments of the bones or other sacred objects belonging to apostles and martyrs – one especially, that of the Holy Cross contain[ed] some relics of the instruments of the passion, and [was] put on exhibition on Good Friday." Statues of the Sacred Heart, St. Anne, and St. Joseph were also located on the main altar with "lights burning daily before them."[42]

The two permanent side altars were dedicated to the Virgin Mary and St. Joseph. Both were constructed "on the same lines as the main altar, and reach[ed] from the floor of the sanctuary to the ceiling." According to Mulkerins, each had three Gothic turrets, two smaller ones on the sides and the main one on top. The side altar dedicated to the Virgin contained a large statue of Our Lady of Lourdes flanked by two smaller statues of St. Aloysius and St. John Berchmans. A picture of the Immaculate Conception hung nearby.[43] The statue of Our Lady of Lourdes was the focus of May devotions in the new church. During May, the "little statue . . . , noted for its devotional beauty, . . . [was] taken down from its niche on the top of the altar and placed in the beautiful shrine prepared for it."[44] The side altar dedicated to St. Joseph contained two pictures, one of St. Charles Borromeo administering holy communion to St. Aloysius, and above it a picture of St. Joseph holding the child Jesus. Statues of St. Aloysius and St. Stanislaus were located on either side of the base of the altar.[45]

Mulkerins reported that in 1873 "new Stations of the Cross were erected." These stations, imported from Europe, were eight feet high and six feet wide. Mulkerins stressed the realistic character of the paintings with their almost life-sized figures each standing out "as if the life blood was coursing through the body."[46] A few other devotions and a variety of new devotional societies were introduced once the congregation moved into the new church. New devotions included devotions to the Sacred Heart of Jesus, an annual solemn novena "in honor of the patronage of St. Joseph,"[47] and the forty hours devotion, which was introduced in 1876.[48]

According to Mulkerins, "the first great mission ever held in Holy Family Parish was begun [in August 1861], and continued for two weeks." Mission exercises included Mass and instruction at five in the morning; Mass and a sermon at eight in the morning; the way of the cross and instruction in the afternoon; and the rosary, a sermon, and benediction of the Blessed Sacrament in the evening.[49]

Another mission was held in 1869 which was "thought, by some, to be perhaps the greatest mission ever given in Holy Family Church." According to Mulkerins, "Fathers Damen, Smarius, Masselis, Coghlan and Verdin [from Holy Family parish] all took part and at least two of these, Fathers Damen and Smarius, were undoubtedly the greatest missionaries in the United States during their day."[50]

New organizations founded in the new church included an

Acolythical Society for boys in 1860; the Association of the Sacred Heart, the Holy Rosary Society, the Young Ladies' Sodality, the Holy Angels' Sodality, and the Society of the Living Rosary in 1861; St. Ann's Sodality for married women and the Married Men's Band in 1862; the Purgatorial Society and the Apostleship of Prayer in 1864; the Sodality of the Annunciation in 1868; Bona Mors Society and the Young Men's Sodality in 1869; and the Catholic Total Abstinence and Benevolent Society in 1870.[51]

Although mid-nineteenth-century American priests spent an enormous amount of time raising money and overseeing the construction of new churches and schools, their obsession with building, viewed from a devotional angle, reflected the immigrant Catholics' desire to create a distinctively Catholic space. For the Romanized Catholic, the parish church was the center of that Catholic space and within the church, the altar with its tabernacle containing the Blessed Sacrament was the center of attention. But the side altars, statues, votive candles, the stained glass, the stations of the cross, and the dim light, all contributed to the creation of a distinctively Catholic interior as well.

A man who had grown up in Holy Family parish captured something of the impact of the church's interior. Returning some years later, he said:

> I noted the seven lights still burning before the statue of the Blessed Virgin, lighted in 1871 by Father Damen, and to be kept forever burning in Her honor in thanksgiving for the preservation of the church and the parish from the ravages of the great fire that all but consumed Chicago. The fine old stations of the Cross still ornament and glorify the walls looking more than ever like old masters. The same majestic altar, the sturdy pews, the roomy confessionals and the strikingly beautiful altar rail, both masterpieces of the wood carver's art, the galaxy of saints and martyrs and confessors all about on their carven pedestals and the soft light filtering through the art windows selected and executed with erudition and devotion, *all conjure up such feelings and emotions as I experience nowhere else—as if it were nearer Heaven here than elsewhere.*[52]

The interior design of the church was intended to conjure up exactly the sort of feelings this returning parishioner described. Catholics were taught that Jesus *was* present on the altar; that Jesus, Mary, and the saints *did* respond to prayer, and that graces and favors *were* more readily available in the church than elsewhere. The devotional artifacts within the church helped to create the sense that one was in a sacred space where familiar intercourse between this world and the other world could take place.

The luxuriant growth of devotional organizations both protected, defined, and directed attention toward this sacred space. In the words of one nineteenth-century prelate, such organizations were designed "to create artificially environments in which the supernatural life could develop freely."[53] While church buildings created a material space for interacting with the supernatural, devotional organizations created a social space in which such activities could be taken for granted. These organizations, the primary arena for intensified adult lay involvement in the church at that time, thus helped maintain the subjective reality of that other, supernatural world with which Catholics communicated through prayer.

Although devotional organizations were at the center of parish life, they were surrounded by a growing network of organizations (mutual benefit, temperance, and charity) and institutions (schools, hospitals, orphanages, and cemeteries) that radiated outward from the church. This growing network of associations and institutions permitted and encouraged Catholics to remain within the confines of the group for all their primary relationships throughout the various stages of their lives.[54]

PIETY AND THE FORMATION OF EXCLUSIVE COMMUNITIES

The Catholic Church was not the only religious group in nineteenth-century America which promoted the growth of religious organizations and fostered more intense forms of piety. With the separation of church and state, all denominations had been forced, as it were, onto the free market. According to Peter Berger:

The key characteristic of all pluralistic situations, whatever the details of their historical background, is that the religious ex-monopolies can no longer take for granted the allegiance of their client populations. Allegiance is voluntary and thus, by definition, less certain. As a result, the religious tradition, which previously could be authoritatively imposed, now must be *marketed*. It must be "sold" to a clientele that is no longer constrained to "buy." The pluralistic situation is, above all, a *market situation*.[55]

While both Protestants and Catholics responded to these demands by attempting to strengthen and intensify lay commitment, they did so in different but analogous ways. Where Catholics held parish missions,[56] promoted popular devotions, established confraternities and sodalities, and emphasized the authority and infallibility of the pope, mid-nineteenth-century evangelical Protestants held revivals,[57] sang gospel hymns,[58] established prayer groups and mission societies, and emphasized the authority and infallibility of the Bible.

While the central devotional symbol of Roman Catholicism was the Blessed Sacrament, the central devotional symbol of Protestantism was the Bible:

> [For Protestants] the essential, imperative exercise of religious life, the one thing not to be omitted, was for everyone the reading of the Bible. This was what the [Protestant] reformers *put in the place of the Mass* as the decisive high point of spiritual experience—instead of participation in the sacrament of the real presence on one's knees in the church, they put encounter with the Holy Spirit in the familiar language of men on the printed page of the sacred text.[59]

Although, as Gerald Fogarty has pointed out, "the [Protestant] charge that Catholics were forbidden to read the Bible was in reality unfounded, . . . circumstances led to the popular conception that the Bible was a Protestant book."[60] For evangelical Protestants and ultramontane Catholics, the Protestant Bible, individually interpreted, and the Blessed Sacrament were thus competing devotional symbols, the former linked to the evangelical emphasis on preaching and the latter linked to the

Roman emphasis on the Mass. Moreover, because of the importance of the Blessed Sacrament, Catholics emphasized the sacrality of the church's interior where Jesus was exposed on the altar, while, because of the importance of lay Bible reading, evangelical Protestants placed an increased emphasis on the sacrality of the home.[61]

The intensity of the affective bonds created within these subcultures, heightened by their distinctive practices and their mutually exclusive understandings of "authentic" Christianity, enhanced their ability to create and maintain group boundaries. As well-bounded groups, they fostered a clear sense of identity for their members. They knew what it meant to belong and what it meant to be an outsider. According to Hugh McLeod, nineteenth-century religious movements typically "made absolute claims for themselves; they combined aggressive evangelism with the attempt to mark out sharp and clear boundaries between their own community and the world beyond. This was the age of the self-built ghettos—Catholic, Protestant, liberal, socialist."[62]

In the United States, evangelical Protestants, nativists, and devotion-minded Catholics all relied upon the language of purity and defilement to express the threat which outside forces posed to the cohesiveness of the group. Where Catholics used devotions to keep heresy from defiling the purity of the church, Protestants, according to Sandra Sizer, "appropriate[d gospel hymns] as symbols of unity in the face of potential threats from groups perceived as alien, whether aristocratic Southerners or despotic Catholics." Protestant evangelicals (like devotion-minded Catholics, I would add) had, in Sizer's words, "a propensity to see conspiracies lurking around every corner."[63] Moreover, "just as revivalists sought to stimulate Christian fellowship by awakening men to the horrors of sin," so nativists, according to David Davis, "used apocalyptic images [of secret conspiracies plotted by Mormons, Masons, and Catholics to undermine American society] to ignite human passions, destroy selfish indifference, and join patriots in a cohesive brotherhood."[64] Nativists seemed, Davis suggests, "at times to recognize an almost beneficent side to subversive organizations, since they joined the nation on a glorious crusade and thus kept it from moral and social disintegration."[65]

Just as the threat of Catholicism was summoned up by Protestants and nativists to foster the cohesiveness of a publicly, if unofficially, Protestant nation, so too the spectre of nativism was called upon by Catholics to reinforce the solidarity of the Catholic subculture. Although nativist hostility may have played a part in the formation of a Catholic subculture, Catholic emphasis on nativism as a cause of subcultural cohesiveness obscures the extent to which mid-nineteenth-century Catholic theology and practice itself fostered the creation of an enclosed Catholic subculture and indeed was able to use nativist hostility to reinforce American Catholics' view of themselves as a beleaguered minority banding together to protect itself from the attacks of its enemies.

As Martin Marty has noted, "when apologists for Catholic behavior and critics of the encircling WASP culture wanted to reinforce and legitimate Catholic group bonding they accentuated the ways in which ghetto life was *imposed upon* minorities":

> At other times during the domestic *aggiornamento* that followed the Second Vatican Council, however, a self-deprecating, indeed sometimes almost masochistic view of the tradition prevailed, then the ghetto was seen not as imposed from without but self-imposed from within.[66]

Thus, the emphasis on nativism as a cause of Catholic subcultural cohesiveness suggests that Catholic communalism was imposed on Catholics, rather than, as I would emphasize, the product of a massive and deliberate community-building effort carried out in a religiously competitive environment.

ROMAN CATHOLIC PIETY AND THE PUBLIC ORDER

So far, I have considered Protestants, nativists, and Catholics as competing and sometimes overlapping groups within

American society. The relationship of Protestants and Catholics to American society as a whole, however, was not symmetrical. Although Catholics made up the largest individual denomination in the United States at mid-century, Protestant denominations, when taken together, outnumbered Catholics by about two to one.[67] Most critically, however, Protestants controlled, and were fighting to maintain control over, the institutions of national or public self-definition. Not surprisingly, the most intense conflict between Catholics and Protestant nativists arose over issues that threatened Protestant hegemony over the institutions and symbols that defined American public life. This is most clearly illustrated by the controversy over Bible-reading in the public schools.

Schools played an important role in the definition of public life in the United States because they were located on the boundary between public and private life. Insofar as schools were run by the state, they were, at least in theory, to be religiously neutral; as critical agents of socialization, they inevitably inculcated values which either supported or undermined those taught by particular families or denominations. Thus, in practice, antebellum American Protestants defined neutrality as nonsectarian Protestantism. According to Timothy Smith:

> By their establishment and control of both public and private schools, [Protestant] churchmen stamped upon neighborhoods, states, and nation an interdenominational Protestant ideology which nurtured dreams of personal and social progress. By the middle of the nineteenth century, leading citizens assumed that Americanism and Protestantism were synonyms and that education and Protestantism were allies. The prevalence of this sentiment encouraged nativism, muted the voice of the courts in issues involving church-state relationships, and impelled Jews, Catholics, and some Protestant groups who rejected the interdenominational consensus to institute separate systems of parochial education.[68]

Catholic attempts to change the public schools began in New York in 1840 and in Philadelphia in 1841, and were revived on a larger scale during the 1850s.[69] The key issue, from

a devotional point of view, was the reading of Protestant translations of the Bible. As indicated above, Bible reading was
a typically Protestant form of devotion, and although Bible
reading was not discouraged by the Catholic hierarchy, Catholics were required to use an authorized translation of the Latin
Vulgate.[70]

Catholic attempts to modify America's public devotional life
– by excluding Bible-reading altogether, by allowing Catholic
teachers and students to read from the Douay version, or by
establishing Catholic schools with public funds – aroused a vehe-
ment nativist response. In fact, according to Hueston:

> A correlation exists between the most severe outbursts of native
> American hostility in the 1840s and 1850s and Irish Catholic cam-
> paigns in behalf of their Church or their native country, campaigns
> which *flaunted the uniqueness of these elements* and directly or in-
> directly challenged established patterns of thought or behavior in
> American society.[71]

Although in some cases concessions were made to Catholic
demands,[72] the hostile reaction of non-Catholics forced Catholic leaders, for the most part, to back away from attempts to re-
define America's public religion. Those bishops who did take
on a public role tended to emphasize the common ground between Protestants and Catholics. The lack of symmetry in Protestant and Catholic relationships to the symbols and institutions
of national self-definition thus forced greater concessions on
Catholics than on Protestants. Catholics could either moderate
their differences with Protestants in order to take on a public
role or assert their distinctiveness privately.

In the first issue of *Ave Maria*, Father Sorin used a familial
metaphor to legitimate the relocation of Catholicism, and particularly the more distinctive and thus to Protestants more dis-
turbing aspects of Catholic belief and practice, within the
Catholic subculture rather than moderating, denying, or attempting to impose them on society as a whole. Urging his American
Catholic readers to think of themselves as one family among
many, he asked them to "imagine a family of children seated

around a cheerful fireside" discussing their neighbors' attitudes toward their mother and how that ought to affect their behavior toward her.

One of the children, Albert, suggests that although they all love their mother very much "we need not talk *too much* about her, even among ourselves, for Mrs. Grundy may overhear us, and we all know she and her family maintain that mother, after all, is only an ordinary sort of woman."[73]

According to Hannah Jane, the Smiths, who "are very rich . . . [and] move in the best society," claim to "know mother much better than we do ourselves, and . . . [declare] that she has no particular affection for any of us." Hannah Jane refutes this as absurd, describing how their mother watches over them, gratifies their wishes, and labors for their happiness, yet concludes that "it would not be well . . . to show her so much outward demonstrations of affection" while visiting their rich and influential neighbors.[74]

Jemima Matilda points out that others, such as Mr. White, do "not even believe *she is our mother.* . . ." She points out that "the Whites are even richer than the Smiths, they are much more intellectual and learned, they understand all the philosophical questions of the age, beside metaphysics; . . . so if we wish to retain their good opinion it will be better, I think, to say—that—*we have no mother.*"[75] Giles, declaring such conduct shameful, wants to refute all these opinions and "even make use of knock-down arguments to vindicate our mother's fair fame."

Finally, however, John rejects all these options, asking "Who, after all are the Whites, the Smiths, and Grundies?" They are, he goes on to say, but "three families of yesterday, who sprang up in our neighborhood like mushrooms." Unlike these newcomers, their Catholic family has a rich heritage:

Think of our princely domain, of our glorious ancestors, of all our other noble brothers and fair sisters, living and dead, who have, with us, the love of our sweet mother. Let us seek those of our own household, and, united with them, testify our love for our dear mother and we will think very little and care still less, for the slanders of the Smiths, the Whites, and the Grundies.[76]

As *Ave Maria* portrayed them, mid-nineteenth-century American Catholics had three options with respect to American society. They could modify or abandon their distinctive religious practices to please others; they could attempt to vindicate their practices in Protestant eyes; or they could band together and ignore what outsiders had to say about them. During the middle decades of the nineteenth century, most American Catholics, under the influence of strong Romanizing tendencies within the church as a whole, chose to assert their distinctiveness in the private sphere rather than moderate their Catholicism for "public" (i.e., non-Catholic) consumption.

The Catholic desire to take distinctively Catholic doctrines such as the real presence and the communion of saints seriously and literally thus had both religious and sociological consequences. Religiously, it led to the generation of numerous devotions designed to foster intense emotional bonds between Catholics and their supernatural "relatives." Sociologically, it nurtured a church-centered form of piety and a sense of communal solidarity. Devotion to Jesus in the Blessed Sacrament and to Mary and the saints, however, was not acceptable as a public symbol of national identity in the same way that reverence toward the Bible was. Rather than abandon that which made them distinctively Catholic or fight what seemed to be a hopeless battle for public religious pluralism, Catholics redefined their devotional life as a "family matter," relocating it within the private sphere.

The enthusiastic adoption of an aggressively Roman form of piety by English-speaking Catholics fostered the rapid institutional growth of the Catholic Church in the United States. In promoting a more intense and exclusive form of Catholicism, mid-nineteenth-century Catholics were, in some ways, more like their evangelical Protestant antagonists than their more accommodating and ecumenically-minded Anglo-Catholic predecessors. Catholics and Protestants differed, however, in their access to the public realm. While the King James Bible, symbol of the Protestant Reformation, was publicly venerated as an American symbol, devotion to the Blessed Sacrament, symbol of the Counter-Reformation, had to be expressed privately, if at all. In a Protestant-dominated environment, Catholics had to choose either to participate in the public realm on largely Protestant terms, which generally meant emphasizing that which they held in common, or celebrating their distinctiveness in private. Most mid-nineteenth-century Catholics chose the latter course, which, naturally enough, tended to enhance their isolation from the dominant culture.

APPENDIX A

Prayer Books Published in the U.S., 1770–1880

1. *The Garden of the Soul*. Philadelphia: Joseph Cruickshank [177–?].
2. *A Manual of Catholic Prayers*. Philadelphia: A. Bell, 1774.
3. *The Devout Christian's Vade-Mecum*. Philadelphia: M. Carey, 1789.
4. *The Pious Guide*. Georgetown, D.C.: James Doyle, 1792.
5. *The Pious Christian Instructed in . . . the Principal Exercises of Piety . . . Bp. Hay*. Philadelphia: M. Carey, 1800.
6. *The Roman Catholic Manual*. Boston: Manning & Loring, 1803.
7. *The Key of Paradise*. Baltimore, 1804. Note: According to Finotti, *The Key to Paradise* (New York, 1816) is the same as *The Key of Paradise*.
8. *True Piety*. Baltimore: Warner & Hanna, 1809.
9. *The Devout Communicant*. Baker. Philadelphia: Bernard Dornin, 1818.
10. *The Christian's Monitor*. William Taylor. New York: W. H. Creagh, 1819.
11. *The Christian's Guide to Heaven*. Philadelphia, 1819.
12. *Catholic Manual*. John Power. Baltimore: F. Lucas [1825?].
13. *Prince Hohenlohe's Prayer Book*. Philadelphia: E. Cummiskey, 1827.
14. *The Catholic Christian's Guide to Heaven*. New York: James Ryan, 1830.
15. *A Manual of Catholic Piety*. Gahan. New York: John Doyle, 1832.
16. *Devout Manual, or Exercises of Piety*. Baltimore, 1833.
17. *The Path to Paradise*. Baltimore: F. Lucas 1834.
18. *Daily Devotion*. Baltimore: F. Lucas, 1834.
19. *The Poor Man's Manual; or, Devout Christian's Daily Companion*. Baltimore: F. Lucas, 1834. Note: The title of the *Poor Man's Man-*

135

ual; or, Devout Christian's Daily Companion was changed to *The Key of Heaven; or, Devout Christian's Daily Companion* (New York: Catholic Publication Society, 1871) by Lawrence Kehoe of the Catholic Publication Society in 1871. See Paul J. Fullam, "The Catholic Publication Society and its Successors, 1866–1916," *Historical Records and Studies*, XLVII (1959): 37.

20. *The Pocket Manual; or, Devout Vade Mecum.* Baltimore: F. Lucas, 1834.
21. *The Layman's Ritual.* New York: John Doyle, 1834.
22. *Ursuline Manual.* Charleston, S.C., 1835.
23. *Daily Exercise.* Baltimore: F. Lucas [1835?].
24. *Catholic Spiritual Prayer Book.* Boston: Chas. T. Young, 1838.
25. *The Key of Heaven.* Milner. Baltimore: F. Lucas [1840?].
26. *The Catholic Companion.* Philadelphia, 1843.
27. *St. Vincent's Manual.* Baltimore: Murphy, 1843.
28. *Daily Companion.* Baltimore: F. Lucas, 1844.
29. *Flowers of Piety.* Baltimore: F. Lucas, 1844.
30. *Pocket Companion.* Baltimore: F. Lucas, 1845.
31. *St. Joseph's Manual.* Baltimore: F. Lucas, 1845.
32. *Gems of Devotion.* Baltimore, 1845.
33. *Chapel Companion.* Baltimore: F. Lucas, 1846.
34. *Visitation Manual.* Baltimore: F. Lucas, 1845. *The Visitation Manual* was also published as *The New Catholic Manual* (Philadelphia: McGrath, 1852) and *The Spirit of Prayer* (Philadelphia: McGrath, 1861), according to advertisements in *The Catholic Directory.*
35. *Catholic Christian's Companion to Prayer, the Sacraments, and the Holy Sacrifice of the Mass.* Baltimore: Murphy, 1848.
36. *Guide to Heaven.* Baltimore: Murphy, 1848.
37. *Christian Sacrifice Illustrated.* Baltimore: Murphy, 1848.
38. *Miniature Key of Heaven and Catholic Christian's Daily Companion.* Baltimore: Murphy, 1848.
39. *Vade Mecum.* New York: Sadlier, 1848.
40. *Carmelite Manual.* 1850.
41. *Manual of the Sacred Heart.* Philadelphia: McGrath, 1850.
42. *Gems of Piety.* Philadelphia: McGrath, 1850.
43. *The Golden Manual.* New York: Sadlier, 1851.
44. *Devotions to Mass Applied to Holy Communion.* Philadelphia: McGrath, 1850.
45. *Daily Piety; A New Prayer Book.* New York: Dunigan, 1851.

46. *Catholic Piety*. Philadelphia: McGrath, 1852.
47. *Key of Heaven*. Fitton. Boston: T. Sweeney, 1852. Note: I suspect that this *Key of Heaven* was only *edited* by Fitton, which might make it equivalent to 25, above.
48. *The Way to Heaven*. New York: Sadlier, 1853.
49. *The Mission Book*. New York: M. T. Cozans, 1853.
50. *The Spirit of Devotion*. Philadelphia: McGrath, 1853.
51. *St. John's Manual*. New York: Dunigan, 1856.
52. *Catholic Hours; or, The Family Prayer Book*. [1856?].
53. *Star of Bethlehem*. New York: O'Shea, 1857.
54. *Little Flowers of Piety*. [1857?].
55. *Miniature Key of Heaven*. Boston: Donahoe, 1857.
56. *The Little Mission Book*. 1858.
57. *The Companion to the Sanctuary*. 1858.
58. *Flower Garden*. Philadelphia: Cunningham, 1858.
59. *Raccolta*. Trans. by Ambrose St. John. New York: Sadlier [1858?]. Note: The introduction to the *Raccolta* states that it is laid out so that it can be used as a prayer book.
60. *Flowers of Paradise*. [Sisters of Mercy.] New York: O'Shea, 1859.
61. *Little Mission Book and Pocket Manual*. Cincinnati, 1859.
62. *Manual of Catholic Devotions*. Baltimore: Murphy, 1859.
63. *The Altar Manual*. New York: Sadlier, 1859.
64. *A Manual of Prayers*. New York: Dunigan, 1859.
65. *Angel of Prayer, with a Selection of Devotions*. Richmond, Va.: Randolph, 1861.
66. *Daily Prayer . . . Adapted to All States*. New York: Sadlier, 1861.
67. *The Mass Book*. New York: Sadlier, 1863.
68. *The Help of Christians*. [Sisters of Mercy.] New York: Sadlier, 1864.
69. *The Little Flower Garden*. Philadelphia: McGrath [1864?].
70. *Sacred Heart Mission Book*. Cincinnati: Walsh [1864?].
71. *Christian's Daily Guide*. New York: O'Shea, 1865.
72. *Catholic's Vade Mecum*. Baltimore: Kelly & Piet, 1865.
73. *Purgation Manual*. New York, 1866.
74. *Crown of Jesus*. [Dominicans.] New York: Dunigan [1869?].
75. *Flowers of Devotion*. Baltimore: Kelly & Piet, 1869.
76. *Little Crown of Jesus*. Baltimore: Kelly & Piet, 1869.
77. *Companion of the Sanctuary*. Boston: Donahoe, 1870.
78. *Pocket Prayer Book*. New York: Catholic Publication Society, 1871.

79. *St. Patrick's Manual.* New York: Sadlier, 1874.
80. *Manual of the Sisters of Charity.* Baltimore: Murphy, 1875.

Comments

Sources: The list was compiled from John Wright, *Early Prayer Books of America*, Catholic University of America; *A Survey of Book Publishing in the United States, 1831–1900;* Joseph Finotti, *Bibliographia Catholica Americana;* and advertisements in *The Catholic Directory.*

Since there were some discrepancies between these lists during the periods of overlap, i.e., to 1820 and from 1830 to 1860, there may be a few titles missing, particularly after 1860.

Books with similar titles were always counted separately unless independent evidence indicated that they were the same book.

Frequency of
Prayer Book Publication

1. *The Garden of the Soul.*
   Philadelphia: Cruickshank, 177–?
   Philadelphia: Carey, 1789, 1792, 1809.
   Baltimore, 1814.
   Baltimore: Lucas, 1834, 1845, 1851, 1860?, 1864? (352 pp.).
   Baltimore: Murphy, 1849.
   New York: Sadlier, 1845, 1847, 1850, 1870, 1871 (448 pp.).
   New York: Catholic Publication Society, 1870.
2. *The Devout Christian's Vade Mecum.*
   Philadelphia: Carey, 1789, 1792, 1797.
   Baltimore: Warner & Hanna, 1801.
   Baltimore: Warner, 1812, 1814.
   New York: Kinnersley, 1813.
   New York: Smith & Forman, 1814.
   Philadelphia: Cummiskey, 1820.
   New York: Phelan, 1840.
   Baltimore: Lucas, 1845.
   Baltimore: Kelly & Piet, n.d.
   New York: Catholic Publication Society, 1871.
3. *The Pious Guide to Prayer and Devotion.*
   Georgetown: Doyle, 1792.
   New York: Dornin, 1808, 1809, 1813, 1815.
   Georgetown: Milligan, 1815, 1825 (389 pp.).
   Baltimore: Lucas, 1827? (387 pp.), 1834, 1842 (457 pp.), 1845,
      1846 (508 pp.), 1847, 1851, 1860?, 187–?
   Cincinnati: Walsh, 1861?
   New York: Catholic Publication Society, 1870, 1875.

4. *The Key of Paradise.*
   Baltimore: Wane & Murphy, 1804 (438 pp.).
   Baltimore: Lucas, 1842, 1845, 1856?
   Baltimore: Murphy, 1848, 1849.
   Philadelphia: Cummiskey, n.d.
   New York: Catholic Publication Society, 1870.
5. *True Piety.*
   Baltimore: Warner & Hanna, 1809 (512 pp.).
   Baltimore: Warner, 1814 (526 pp.).
   Philadelphia: Cummiskey, 1824, 1826, 1832.
   Lexington: Kentucky Gazette Office, 1824 (repr. of 1809 ed.).
   Georgetown: Milligan, 1825.
   Baltimore: Murphy, 1848.
   Baltimore: Lucas, n.d. (463 pp.).
   New York: Catholic Publication Society, n.d.
6. *The Christian's Guide to Heaven.*
   Philadelphia, 1819.
   Philadelphia: LeBreton, 1826 (350 pp.).
   Baltimore: Lucas, 1829 (351 pp.), 1834, 1844, n.d. (383 pp.).
   Philadelphia: McGrath, 1849, 1853, 1864?
   Boston: Donahoe, 1849.
   Baltimore: Murphy, 1849.
   New York: Benziger, 1864?
   Baltimore: Kelly & Piet, 1869.
   Philadelphia: Cummiskey, 187–?
   New York: Catholic Publication Society, 1870 (382 pp.).
7. *Catholic Manual.*
   Baltimore: Lucas, 1825? (464 pp.), 1834, 1844, 1845, 1846, 1856?
   New York: Ryan, 1832.
   Baltimore: Murphy, 1849.
   New York: Catholic Publication Society, 1870 (468 pp.).
8. *Prince Hohenlohe's Prayer Book.*
   Baltimore: Myres, 1827 (335 pp.).
   Philadelphia: Cummiskey, 1827.
   Baltimore: Lucas, 1834 (446 pp.), 1845.
9. *The Pocket Manual of Spiritual Exercises.*
   Philadelphia: Cummiskey, 1827.
   Baltimore: Lucas, 1834, 1841, 1845, 1847.
   New York: Sadlier, 1861?

10. *A Manual of Catholic Piety.* Gahan.
    Georgetown: Doyle, 1832.
    Baltimore: Lucas, 1844.
    Philadelphia: McGrath, 1852.
    New York: Dunigan, 1857.
    Boston: Donahoe, 1861.
    Philadelphia: Cunningham, 1875.
    Philadelphia: Cummiskey, n.d.
    New York: Strong, n.d.
    New York: O'Shea, n.d.
11. *Devout Manual.*
    Baltimore, 1833.
    Baltimore: Myres, 1834.
    New York: Dunigan, 1842 (384 pp.), 1851, 1857 (540 pp.).
    Baltimore: Hedian, 1857.
12. *Path to Paradise.*
    Baltimore: Lucas, 1834, 1844.
    Baltimore: Murphy, 1849.
    New York: Sadlier, 1864, 1875.
    New York, 1878.
    New York: Catholic Publication Society, n.d.
13. *Poor Man's Manual = Key of Heaven.*
    Baltimore: Lucas, 1834, 1841, 1850.
    New York: Catholic Publication Society, 1870, 1871, 1880.
14. *The Daily Exercise.*
    Baltimore: Lucas, 1835?, 1844, 1845, 1846, 1847.
    Baltimore: Murphy, 1848, 1849, 1880.
    Boston: Donahoe, 1849, 1862.
    New York: Benziger, 1864?, 1871.
    Boston: Noonan, 1873.
    New York: O'Shea, n.d.
    Philadelphia: Cunningham, n.d.
15. *Ursuline Manual = New Manual of Catholic Devotion = The Spirit
    of Prayer.*
    Charleston, 1835, 1840.
    New York: Dunigan, 1840 (520 pp.), 1845, 1848, 1851, 1857 (520
    pp.), 1857 (864 pp.).
    New York: Kelly, 1840 (2nd Am. ed., 578 pp.).
    Baltimore: Lucas, 1841, 1844, 1845, 1846, 1847.

New York: Kenedy, 1851 (864 pp.).

Philadelphia: McGrath, 1851, 1852, 1855, 1861, 1864?

16. *The Key of Heaven, or, A Manual of Prayers.* Milner.

Baltimore: Lucas, 1840?, 1844, 1845.

New York: Kirker, 1858.

New York: O'Shea, 1860, 1873.

Boston: Donahoe, 1862.

Baltimore: Murphy, 1867 (480 pp.), 1876, 1880 (480 pp.), 1882 (707 pp.).

New York: Kenedy, 1867 (512 pp.), 1870 (683 pp.).

New York: Sadlier, 1869?, 1874 (671 pp.), 1875 (426 pp.).

Boston: Noonan, 1873 (525 pp.).

New York: Kelly, 1874 (736 pp.).

The Key of Heaven, a Manual of Devout Prayers, for Daily Use.

Baltimore: Kelly & Piet, 1870 (386 pp.).

The Key of Heaven, or, A Manual of Prayer for the Use of the Faithful.

New York: Benziger, 1879 (422 pp.).

17. *St. Vincent's Manual.*

Baltimore: Murphy, 1843, 1848, 1849, 1850, 1851, 1852, 1853, 1854, 1856, 1857, 1859, 1860, 1862.

18. *St. Joseph's Manual.*

Baltimore: Lucas, 1845.

Boston: Donahoe, 1853, 1862 (696 pp.).

Boston: Noonan, 1877 (819 pp.).

19. *The Guide to Heaven.*

Baltimore: Murphy, 1848.

Philadelphia: McGrath, 1851.

Boston: Donahoe, 1859, 1862.

Philadelphia: Cummiskey, 1862.

20. *The Golden Manual.*

New York: Sadlier, 1851, 1852, 1858, 1859, 1863, 1864, 1867, 1872.

21. *The Mission Book.*

New York: Cozans, 1853.

New York: O'Shea, 1853, 1860, 1867 (498 pp.).

New York: Sadlier, 1853 (500 pp.), 1862, 1863 (500 pp.).

New York: Dunigan, 1854, 1857 (490 pp.), 1858.

New York, 1854.

Baltimore: Kelly, Hedian, & Piet, 1863 (502 pp.).
New York: Kirker, 1864?
New York: Sadlier, 1861, 1862, 1864, 1868.
Philadelphia: Cummiskey, 1870?
New York: Catholic Publication Society, 1871.
Baltimore: Kelly & Piet, n.d.
Boston: Donahoe, n.d.
Boston: Noonan, n.d.
22. *Daily Prayers.*
   New York: Sadlier, 1861, 1862, 1864, 1868.
23. *The Catholic's Vade Mecum.*
   Baltimore: Kelly & Piet, 1865.
   Philadelphia: Cummiskey, 1866, 1873?
   New York: Greil & Wilderman, 1866.
   New York: Catholic Publication Society, 1879?

Comments

In the absence of a recognized international copyright law in the United States prior to 1890, many American publishers pirated European works without paying royalties. (Tebbel, 2: 640). Once a book had been pirated, there was no way to keep other publishers from issuing it as well. As a result, some books, presumably the most popular, were published by numerous firms. In addition, publishers tended to record a new date of publication for each press run of a book.

The sources used to compile this list recorded subsequent dates of publication. Republication data for all prayer books with more than three imprint dates as of 1880 are given here. Additional information on the titles was obtained from the *National Union Catalog* and advertisements in *The Catholic Directory*. Advertisements did not specify dates of republication, but they often supplied additional publishers of a work. In these cases, the publisher is noted without a date of publication. Finally, a few books entered this more selective list because copies with additional imprint dates were found when searching libraries for prayer books.

The data given in this appendix allow us to identify the top-selling prayer books by decade and overall between 1840 and 1880. The number of reprints are indicated in brackets:

BEST-SELLERS, BY DECADE

OVERALL BEST-SELLERS, 1840–80

40s *Ursuline Manual* [10]
 Daily Exercise [7]
50s *St. Vincent's Manual* [8]
 Ursuline Manual [7]
 Mission Book [7]
60s *Mission Book* [6]
 Key of Heaven [5]
70s *Key of Heaven* [7]

Ursuline Manual [19]
Mission Book [18]
Key of Heaven [16]
Daily Exercise [14?]
St. Vincent's Manual [13]
Garden of the Soul [11]
Christian's Guide to Heaven [11]
The Pious Guide [10]
The Golden Manual [8]

APPENDIX C

Prayer Books Examined

Key

* = Prayer book tabulated in Table 6
X = Prayer book tabulated as X in Appendix D
□ = Prayer book tabulated as □ in Appendix D

1. Challoner, Richard. *The Garden of the Soul: A Manual of Spiritual Exercises and Instructions for Christians Who, Living in the World, Aspire to Devotion,* 177–?
   * X Philadelphia: Carey, 1792 (357 pp.); Evans no. 24184.
   □ New York: Sadlier, 1871 (448 pp., 108 pp., 36 pp.). Title page adds: ". . . *with an explanation of the Mass, by the Late Bishop England.* Enlarged edition with the Epistles and Gospels."
2. *The Devout Christian's Vade Mecum,* 1789.
   * X New York: Smith and Forman, 1814 (254 pp.). This edition entitled *The Roman Catholic Prayer Book or, Devout Christian's Vade Mecum.* The contents are the same, according to Finotti, p. 249.
3. *The Pious Guide to Prayer and Devotion,* 1792.
   * X Georgetown: Doyle, 1792 (282 pp.); Evans no. 24695.
   □ Baltimore: Lucas, n.d. (467 pp.). Same as 1842 revision.
4. *The Key of Paradise, Opening the Gate to Eternal Salvation,* 1804.
   * X Baltimore: Wane and Murphy, 1804 (438 pp.).
5. *True Piety, or the Day Well Spent,* 1809.
   X Philadelphia: Cummiskey, 1824.
   * □ Lexington: Kentucky Gazette Office, 1824. Reprint of 1809 edition.
6. *The Christian's Guide to Heaven,* 1819.
   * X New York: Catholic Publication Society, 1870 (382 pp.). Reprint of Lucas edition from 1834 or 1844.

145

7. *The Catholic Manual*, 1825?
   ⋆ X Baltimore: Lucas, 1825?
8. *Prince Hohenlohe's Prayer Book*, 1827.
   ⋆ X Baltimore, Lucas, n.d.
9. *The Pocket Manual*, 1827.
   ⋆ X Philadelphia: Cummiskey, 1827.
10. Gahan, William. *The Manual of Catholic Piety*, 1832.
    ⋆ X Philadelphia: Cummiskey, n.d. (1873?, 384 pp.).
11. *The Devout Manual; or, A Collection of Prayers*, 1883.
    ⋆ X New York: Dunigan, 1842 (384 pp.).
12. *The Path to Paradise; or, The Way of Salvation*, 1834.
    ⋆ X New York: Sadlier, 1864 (512 pp.).
13. *The Poor Man's Manual and Poesy of Prayers; or, The Key of Heaven.*
    ⋆ X Dublin: Hoey, 1796 (333 pp.).
    The Poor Man's Manual of Devotion; or, Devout Christian's Daily Companion, 1834.
       No copies located.
    The Key of Heaven; or, The Devout Christian's Daily Companion. To Which is Added Daily Devotions, or Profitable Manner of Hearing Mass. Also the Complete Mass in Latin and English, and the Epistles and Gospels.
    ☐ New York: Catholic Publication Society, 1880.
14. *The Daily Exercise*, 1835?
    ⋆ X Baltimore: Murphy, 1879.
15. *The Ursuline Manual*, 1840 (Introduced to a lay audience).
    New York: Dunigan, 1840 (520 pp.).
    ⋆ X New York: Dunigan, 1857 (520 pp.).
    ☐ New York: Kenedy, 1902 (864 pp.). Revised in 18__.
16. Milner, John. *The Key of Heaven; or, A Manual of Prayer*, 1840?
    X Dublin: Coyne, 1839.
    ⋆ ☐ Baltimore: Murphy, 1880 (480 pp.) = 1867 ed.
    New York: O'Shea, 1873? Similar to Murphy's 1867 ed.
17. *St. Vincent's Manual*, 1843?
    Baltimore: Murphy, 1850 (787 pp.).
    X Baltimore: Murphy, 1854 (787 pp.).
    ⋆ ☐ Baltimore: Murphy, 1859 (966 pp.).
18. Fitton, James. *St. Joseph's Manual*, 1845?
    ⋆ X Boston: Noonan, 1877 (830 pp.).

19. *The Guide to Heaven,* 1848.
    Not listed in the National Union Catalog.
20. *The Golden Manual, being a Guide to Catholic Devotion, Public and Private, Compiled from approved Sources.*
    London: Burns & Lambert, 1850 (759 pp.).
    New York: Sadlier, 1863 (1041 pp.). No significant changes in English edition.
    * X New York: Sadlier, 1867 (1041 pp.).
21. *The Mission Book,* 1853.
    * X Baltimore: Kelly & Piet, 1862. Reprinted by Arno Press, 19–.
    New York: Sadlier, 1863 (500 pp.). No significant changes.
22. *Daily Prayers: A Manual of Catholic Devotion, compiled from the most approved sources and adapted to all states and conditions of life.*
    New York: Sadlier, 1862.
    * X New York: Sadlier, 1868.
23. *The Catholic's Vade Mecum,* 1865?
    * X Philadelphia: Cummiskey, 1873?
    London: Burns, Oates & Co., 1886? (500 pp.).

Comments

Attempts were made to acquire copies of the twenty-three most frequently issued prayer books. Twenty-two of these titles were obtained, in many cases in more than one edition. One is not listed in the *National Union Catalog* and thus could not be acquired.

APPENDIX D

Devotions in the Most Popular Prayer Books, by Book

Prayer Books Published before 1840: columns 1–14 · **After 1840**: columns 15–23

Devotion	1	2	3	4	5	6	7	8	9	10	11	12	13	14	15	16	17	18	20	21	22	23
Rosary (common)	X	X	X	X	X	X	X	X		X	X	X	X	X	X	X	X	X	X	X	X	X
Other Rosaries	□	X	X	X	X		X	X		X		X	□	X	X	X	X		X	X	X	X
Benediction of Bl. Sac.	X	X	□		X	X	X	X		X		X	□	X	□	X	X			X	X	X
Sacred Heart of Jesus		X		□		X	X			X				X	X	X	X	X	X		X	X
Passion	□	X		□	X							X			X	X			X	X	X	
Bl. Sac.—Visits, Other	□	X		X		X	X								□	X	X	X	X	X	X	X
Happy Death		X				X	X	X							X	□	X		X	X	X	X
St. Joseph		X				X	X								□	X	X	X	X	X	X	
Agnus Dei		X		□							X	X			□	X		X			X	X
Sacred Heart of Mary		X		□		X	X								X		X	X	X			X
St. Aloysius		X				X									X	□	X	X	X			
Crucifixion		X				X						X			□		X				X	X
Litanies	aD	b	bC		bC	b	d	b	?	b	b		bB	b	cD	cB	d	b	d	b	b	d
Novenas	aC		cC		bA			c							cC		c	c	c			
Spec. Days of Week			X	X	X	X									X	X		X	X			
Pious Organizations		X													X		X					X
The Way of the Cross										X		□			□	X	X	X	X	X	X	X
Scapular (Mt. Carmel)										X					□	X	X	X	X			
Souls in Purgatory			□				X								□	X				X	X	X
Immaculate Conception				X											□	□			X		X	X
Seven Dolors of Mary								X							X	X		X	X			X
Infant/Child Jesus						X									X				X	X		X
Forty Hours Devotion															□	□			X	X		X
Other Scapulars																		□		X	X	
Special Months																X						
Confirmation	□		□	X		X	X		X	X	X				X				X	X		
Meditation/Ment Pr	X		□	X	□		X			X	X				X		X	X		X		
First Communion										X					X							

KEY

Prayer books numbered as in Appendix C.
X = Devotion in an earlier edition.
□ = Devotion added to a later edition.
For the specific edition tabulated, see Appendix C.

LITANY CODE for X, a = 0, b < 5, c < 10, d = 10 or more
for □, A = 0, B < 5, C < 10, D = 10 or more
NOVENA CODE for X, a = 0, b < 4, c = 4 or more
for □, A = 0, B < 4, C = 4 or more

Comments

The Ursuline Manual, originally published in 1835 for use in the
Ursuline Convent School in South Carolina, was grouped with the
post-1840 prayer books since it was first published for a general audience in 1840. The specific editions tabulated in this appendix are
marked with an asterisk in Appendix C.

The seven words of Jesus on the cross, the Precious Blood, and
the five wounds, three devotions which appeared infrequently, are
grouped under the heading "crucifixion." A prayer book with one or
more of these devotions counted as containing crucifixion devotions.

Litanies and novenas were recorded generically and not according
to content. A novena to the Sacred Heart, for example, was entered
under "novenas," but not under "Sacred Heart." Because the number of novenas and litanies included in the prayer books varied so
widely, only those prayer books containing more than ten litanies and
more than three novenas were scored in table 6.

Confraternities and sodalities were entered under "pious organizations" and not under the particular devotion which they fostered.

Notes

PREFACE

1. Joseph Wissel, *The Redemptorist on the American Missions*, 3 vols. (3d ed., privately printed, 1920; reprint ed., New York: Arno Press, 1978), 1:52.

1. THE POPULARIZATION OF DEVOTIONAL LITERATURE

1. Charles E. Hambrick-Stowe, *The Practice of Piety: Puritan Devotional Disciplines in Seventeenth-Century New England* (Chapel Hill: University of North Carolina Press, 1982), pp. 25–39.
2. Leonard I. Sweet, "The Evangelical Tradition in America," in Sweet, ed., *The Evangelical Tradition in America* (Macon, Ga.: Mercer University Press, 1984), pp. 45–46.
3. Henry F. Browne, "American Catholic History: A Progress Report on Research and Study," *Church History* 26 (1957): 372–80; David J. O'Brien, "American Catholic Historiography: A Post-Conciliar Evaluation," *Church History* 37 (1968): 80–94.
4. Browne, p. 374.
5. Jay P. Dolan, *Catholic Revivalism: The American Experience, 1830–1900* (Notre Dame: University of Notre Dame Press, 1978).
6. Elizabeth L. Eisenstein, *The Printing Press as an Agent of Change: Communications and Cultural Transformation in Early-Modern Europe*, 2 vols. (Cambridge: Cambridge University Press, 1979), 1: 166–67.
7. Jean Daniélou, A. H. Conratin, and John Kent, *Historical Theology* (London: The Pelican Guide to Modern Theology, 1969), p. 233, quoted in Eisenstein, 1:314.
8. Carl Dehne, "Popular Devotions," *Worship* 49 (1975):449.

9. Eisenstein, 1:390.

10. Arthur Geoffrey Dickens, *The Counter-Reformation* (London: Harcourt, Brace & World, 1969), p. 28, quoted in Eisenstein, 1:315.

11. Jean Delumeau, *Catholicism Between Luther and Voltaire: A New View of the Counter-Reformation*, with an Introduction by John Bossy (Philadelphia: Westminster Press, 1977), pp. 166–68.

12. Donal Kerr emphasizes the role of books in the transition from "native devotions" to "Counter-Reformation spirituality" in early nineteenth-century Ireland. While "native devotions" were most common in the rural areas, Counter-Reformation spirituality, he says "was to have its base in the towns and, as its vehicle, the printed prayerbook in English" (Donal Kerr, "The Early Nineteenth Century: Patterns of Change" [in Irish spirituality], in *Irish Spirituality*, ed. Michael Maher [Dublin: Veritas Publications, 1981], p. 137).

13. John William Tebbel, *A History of Book Publishing in the United States*, 4 vols. (New York: R. R. Bowker Co., 1972–1981), 1: 209, 241–45.

14. Prayer books were not the same as missals, which contained only the official Latin liturgical texts. Even though the *Roman Missal* was published in an English translation as early as 1822, it was not, by and large, used as a prayer book by the laity. According to Francis J. Weber, *The Roman Missal* was prepared for publication by Bishop John England of Charleston. Archbishop Marechal and, through him, Roman officials, were concerned that England was attempting a new translation, when in fact he was only borrowing from already approved translations. However, according to Weber, "it was too late, by the time the missal was fully exonerated, to effectively offset the negative image implanted in the public mind by Roman officials and certain of Bishop England's less talented, but more influential episcopal confrères. Though the 1822 *Roman Missal* represented a giant step forward in the nation's liturgical life, the circumstances of its birth mitigated against the book's wide circulation, at least in the initial edition" (Francis J. Weber, *America's Catholic Heritage: Some Bicentennial Reflections, 1776–1976* [Boston: St. Paul Editions, 1976], pp. 31–33).

15. Joseph M. Finotti, *Bibliographia Catholica Americana: A List of Works Written by Catholic Authors and Published in the United States* (1872; reprint ed., New York: Burt Franklin, 1971); Wilfrid Parsons, *Early Catholic Americana: A List of Books and Other Works by Catholic Authors in the United States, 1729–1830* (New York: Macmillan,

1939); John Wright, *Early Prayer Books of America: Being a Descriptive Account of Prayer Books Published in the United States, Mexico, and Canada* (St. Paul, Minn.: John Wright, 1896); and Catholic University of America, Department of Library Science, *A Survey of Catholic Book Publishing in the United States, 1831–1900* (11 volumes on microfilm, hereafter cited as CUA *Survey*).

16. Donal Kerr mentions a number of prayer books which were popular in mid-nineteenth-century Ireland. These included *The Garden of the Soul* and *The Key of Heaven*, both of which originated in England, and *The Ursuline Manual*, which originated in Ireland. All three of these books were also very popular in the United States during the same period (see Appendix B) (Kerr, pp. 139–40).

17. In compiling the list children's books, republications, and undated listings were excluded.

18. Figures (rounded to the nearest 10,000), are derived from Gerald Shaughnessy, *Has the Immigrant Kept the Faith?* (New York: Arno Press, 1969), pp. 123, 131, 134, 140, and 145.

19. Wright, p. 452.

20. Advertisements in *The Catholic Directory* indicate the prices asked for the prayer books.

21. Lee Soltow and Edward Stevens, *The Rise of Literacy and the Common School in the United States: A Socioeconomic Analysis to 1870* (London and Chicago: University of Chicago Press, 1981), p. 200.

22. Soltow and Stevens, p. 91. See also Stanley K. Schultz, *The Culture Factory: Boston's Public Schools, 1789–1860* (New York: Oxford University Press, 1973), p. 258; Carl F. Kaestle, *The Evolution of an Urban School System: New York City, 1750–1850* (Cambridge: Harvard University Press, 1973), p. 110; idem, *Pillars of the Republic: Common Schools and American Society, 1780–1860* (New York: Hill and Wang, 1983), pp. 70–72.

23. Robert D. Cross, "Origins of the Catholic Parochial Schools in America," *The American Benedictine Review* 16 (1965): 196.

24. Patrick John Dowling, *A History of Irish Education: A Study in Conflicting Loyalties* (Cork: Mercier Press, 1971), pp. 116–21.

25. Kerr, p. 139.

26. Soltow and Stevens, p. 189.

27. They note that "among foreign born women there was greater disparity, and illiteracy rates for foreign born women in the North were two to four times as large as for native born women. While native born women (particularly in urban areas) were rapidly achieving

equality of literacy with native born men, traditional female and familial roles among foreign born women acted to curb equality of literacy between foreign born men and women" (ibid., p. 199).

28. Ibid., pp. 144, 199.

29. Harvey J. Graff, *The Literacy Myth: Literacy and Social Structure in the Nineteenth-Century City* (New York: Academic Press, 1979), p. 58.

30. Ibid., p. 59.

31. "Catholic Literature and the Catholic Public," *Catholic World* 12 (December 1870):405.

32. Jay P. Dolan, *Catholic Revivalism: The American Experience, 1830–1900* (Notre Dame: University of Notre Dame Press, 1978), pp. 12–13.

33. Ibid., pp. 14–15.

34. John V. Mentag, "Catholic Spiritual Revivals, Parish Missions in the Midwest to 1865" (Ph.D. dissertation, Loyola University, 1957), pp. 3–4.

35. John F. Byrne, *The Redemptorist Centenaries* (Philadelphia: The Dolphin Press, 1932), p. 261.

36. Dolan, p. 38.

37. Byrne, pp. 268, 277.

38. Walter Elliott, *The Life of Father Hecker*, 2d ed. (New York: Columbus Press, 1894), p. 326.

39. Gilbert J. Garraghan, *The Jesuits of the Middle United States*, 3 vols. (New York: America Press, 1938), 2:202.

40. Cassian J. Yuhaus, *Compelled to Speak: The Passionists in America, Origin and Apostolate* (Westminster, Md.: Newman Press, 1967), pp. 258, 268, 319.

41. "The Second Plenary Council of Baltimore and Ecclesiastical Discipline in the United States," reprinted from *Les Etudes Religieuses* in *The Catholic World* 9 (July 1869):508.

42. Robert C. Healy, *A Catholic Book Chronicle: The Story of P. J. Kenedy and Sons, 1826–1951* (New York: P. J. Kenedy & Sons, 1951), pp. 31–32.

43. *The Catholic Directory*, 1873.

44. Letter from Damen to Beckx, quoted in Garraghan, 2:100.

45. Sean J. Connolly, *Priests and People in Pre-Famine Ireland, 1780–1845* (New York: St. Martin's Press, 1982), pp. 92–93.

46. *U. S. Catholic Miscellany*, December 8, 1824, quoted in Camil-

lus P. Maes, *The Life of Rev. Charles Nerinckx* (Cincinnati: Robert Clarke & Co., 1880), pp. 163–65.

47. Thomas W. Spalding, *Martin John Spalding, American Churchman* (Washington, D.C.: Catholic University of America, 1973), p. 5.

48. M[artin] J. Spalding, *Sketches of the Early Catholic Missions of Kentucky, from their Commencement in 1787, to the Jubilee of 1826–7* (Louisville: B. J. Webb & Bro., 1844; reprint ed., New York: Arno Press, 1972), p. 145.

49. Rev. W. J. Howlett, *Life of Rev. Charles Nerinckx: Pioneer Missionary of Kentucky and Founder of the Sisters of Loretto at the Foot of the Cross* (Techny, Ill.: The Mission Press, 1915), p. 213.

50. Bernice Wolff [Sister Mary Florence], *The Sodality Movement in the United States, 1926–36* (St. Louis: The Queen's Work, 1939), pp. 21–22.

51. This figure was taken from pp. 7–9 of a computer printout of project data from the Parish History Project run on June 9, 1982. This total differs from the total of 894 parishes given in the project report cited below. The number of parishes founded before 1900 was, however, the same in both cases.

52. Jay P. Dolan and Jeffrey Burns, "The Parish History Project: A Descriptive Analysis of Data" (Cushwa Center, University of Notre Dame, 1983), pp. 2–3 (typewritten). Thirty-nine percent of the parishes founded prior to 1900 could be assigned to no specific ethnic group; 38 percent were German, 11 percent were Irish; 5 percent mixed; and the rest, other. These and other figures which follow were calculated using Dolan and Burns's data (available on tape and computer printout) for the 719 churches founded prior to 1900. In using their data, I have assumed that the Irish and mixed parishes as well as the parishes assigned to no specific ethnic group (hereafter NSG) were all English-speaking. References to "English-speaking parishes" refer to Irish, mixed, and NSG parishes.

53. This figure was obtained by dividing the number of devotional organizations founded in NSG, Irish, and mixed parishes prior to 1900 by the number of NSG, Irish, and mixed parishes founded prior to 1900. The same was done with the German parishes.

54. Twenty-two percent of all devotional organizations founded between 1820 and 1840 were in English-speaking parishes, as compared with 29 percent between 1840 and 1860, 32 percent between 1860 and 1880, and 47 percent between 1880 and 1900.

2. The Rise of Devotionalism

1. Donald Attwater, ed., *A Catholic Dictionary*, 3d ed. (New York: Macmillan Co., 1961), s.v. "Liturgy."

2. Ibid., s.v. "Devotions, Popular." According to Attwater, "the most notable are devotion to the Blessed Sacrament and to the Sacred Heart . . . , to our Lady (especially as immaculately conceived, and as having appeared at Lourdes), to St. Joseph, to St. Antony of Padua . . . ; the use of the rosary and other chaplets of beads; of the stations of the cross; of the monthly devotions; the wearing of scapulars and medals; the observance of the Nine Fridays, etc." Except for St. Anthony and the observance of the Nine Fridays, his list reflects the devotions popularized at mid-century.

3. Ibid.

4. Ibid.

5. Attwater states that liturgical worship "in an extended sense . . . includes the private use of public worship, e.g., nuns singing Office in their private chapel, an individual reciting it to himself on the top of a bus. . . . " (ibid., s.v. "Liturgical Worship").

6. Robert C. Broderick, ed., *The Catholic Encyclopedia* (Nashville: Thomas Nelson Pub., 1976), s.v. "Paraliturgical Actions."

7. See chapter 5, below.

8. Tebbel, 2:675.

9. For a description of how this was done, see Appendix B.

10. A list of the prayer book titles and editions examined is given in Appendix C.

11. For details on how this was done and a breakdown of the devotions in each particular prayer book, see Appendix D.

12. The titles were tabulated by type of devotion. Double entries were made only when a book treated two distinct devotions, e.g., *The Rosary and Scapular Book* was entered under both "rosary" and "scapular" but not under "Mary." Confraternities and sodalities—here listed separately—and novenas were again entered generically, not under the object of devotion.

13. Henry Charles Lea, *A History of Auricular Confession and Indulgences in the Latin Church*, 3 vols. (Philadelphia: Lea Bros. & Co., 1896), 3:542.

14. Sadlier's advertisement in *The Metropolitan Catholic Almanac, and Laity's Directory* (Baltimore: Fielding Lucas, Jr., 1854), p. 40 (of Sadlier's advertising supplement).

15. Ibid., p. 41 (of Sadlier's advertising supplement).

16. Murphy's advertisement in *The Metropolitan Catholic Almanac, and Laity's Directory* (Baltimore: Fielding Lucas, Jr., 1855), p. 18 (of Murphy's advertising supplement).

17. Herbert Thurston, "The Benediction of the Blessed Sacrament," *The Month* 97 (June 1901):596.

18. *The New Catholic Encyclopedia* (hereafter *NCE*), s.v. "Benediction of the Blessed Sacrament," by M. Burbach.

19. Thurston, p. 286.

20. Guilday, pp. 210, 256, 263–64.

21. Garraghan, 2:96–97.

22. *The Mission Book of the Congregation of the Most Holy Redeemer* (Baltimore: Kelly & Piet, 1862; reprint ed., New York: Arno Press, 1978), pp. 401–2.

23. Bernard Dompnier, "Un Aspect de la dévotion eucharistique dans la France du XVIIᵉ siècle: Les prières des Quarante-Heures," *Revue d'histoire de l'église de France* 67 (1981):6–9.

24. There are scattered references to the devotion before 1850. It is mentioned in a Philadelphia synodical statute in 1832, and was celebrated in 1839 by the Redemptorists in a church in Peru, Ohio. See Hugh J. Nolan, *The Most Reverend Francis Patrick Kenrick, Third Bishop of Philadelphia, 1830–1851* (Washington, D.C.: Catholic University of America Press, 1948), p. 146, and Roger Aubert, *The Church in a Secularized Society* (New York: Paulist Press, 1978), p. 278.

25. Michael J. Curley, *Venerable John Neumann, C.SS.R., Fourth Bishop of Philadelphia* (Washington, D.C.: Catholic University of America Press, 1952), pp. 219–20.

26. Thomas W. Spalding, *Martin John Spalding: American Churchman* (Washington, D.C.: Catholic University of America Press, 1973), p. 191. There are references to the spread of the forty hours devotion during the 1860s in *The Mission Book*, p. 401, and Thomas J. Callahan, ed., *The Diary of Richard Burtsell, Priest of New York: The Early Years, 1865–1868* (New York: Arno Press, 1978), p. 54.

27. Alphonsus Liguori, *Complete Ascetical Works of St. Alphonsus Liguori*, ed. Eugene Grimm, vol. 6: *The Holy Eucharist*, 3d ed. (Brooklyn: Redemptorist Fathers, 1934), p. 123.

28. *The Raccolta, or, Collection of Prayers and Good Works to Which the Sovereign Pontiffs Have Attached Holy Indulgences.* Published by order of his holiness, Pope Pius IX. Translated, authorized, and ap-

proved by the Sacred Congregation of Holy Indulgences. (Woodstock, Md.: Woodstock College, 1878), pp. 119–20, 128, 141.

29. *St. Vincent's Manual* (Baltimore: John Murphy, 1854; hereafter *St. Vincent's Manual* [1854], p. 606.

30. Thomas J. Mulkerins, *Holy Family Parish, Chicago*, ed. Joseph J. Thompson (Chicago: Universal Press, 1923), pp. 668–69.

31. Herbert Thurston, "The Stations of the Cross," *The Month* 96 (Aug. 1900): 162, and (Sept. 1900): 293.

32. *The Raccolta*, p. 103.

33. *The Mission Book*, p. 127, and Andrew Arnold Lambing, *The Sacramentals of the Holy Catholic Church*, 2d ed. (New York: Benziger Bros., 1896), pp. 83–84.

34. Joseph Wissel, *The Redemptorist on the American Missions*, 3d ed., 3 vols. (privately printed, 1920; reprint ed., New York: Arno Press, 1978), 2:36–37; John Talbot Smith, *The Catholic Church in New York: A History of the New York Diocese From its Establishment in 1808 to the Present Time* (New York and Boston: Hall & Locke Co. 1905), p. 317; and Garraghan, 2:96.

35. *The Catholic Encyclopedia* (hereafter *CE*), s.v. "Heart of Jesus, Devotion to," by Jean Bainvel. For a detailed discussion of medieval mysticism and the Sacred Heart of Jesus, see Josef Stierli, "Devotion to the Sacred Heart From the End of Patristic Times Down to St. Margaret Mary," in Stierli, *The Heart of the Saviour: A Symposium on Devotion to the Sacred Heart* (New York: Herder & Herder, 1958), pp. 59–107. For the history of the official recognition of Sacred Heart devotions, see *CE*, s.v. "Heart of Jesus, Devotion to," by Bainvel; Joseph de Guibert, *The Jesuits: Their Spiritual Doctrine and Practice, A Historical Study*, ed. George E. Ganss (Chicago: Institute of Jesuit Sources, 1964), p. 398; and Josef Stierli, "The Development of the Church's Devotion to the Sacred Heart in Modern Times," in *The Heart of the Saviour*, pp. 109–30.

36. Jacques Le Brun, "Politics and Spirituality: The Devotion to the Sacred Heart," in *The Concrete Christian Life*, ed. Christian Duquoc (New York: Herder & Herder, 1971), pp. 38–39.

37. See, e.g., *St. Vincent's Manual* [1854], pp. 350–51.

38. "June, the Month of the Sacred Heart," *Ave Maria* 2 (June 2, 1866): 340.

39. *CE*, s.v. "Visits to the Blessed Sacrament," by Herbert Thurston.

40. In 1874, Orestes Brownson, who was not particularly fond of

the devotion, described it as "just now the fashionable devotion" (Brownson, "Answer to Objections," *Brownson's Quarterly Review* [Oct. 1874], in *The Works of Orestes A. Brownson*, 20 vols., ed. Henry Brownson [Detroit: Thorndike Nourse Pub., 1882–1887; hereafter Brownson's *Works*], 20:419). In his history of the diocese of New York, John Talbot Smith indicates that Sacred Heart devotions eclipsed the forty hours devotion in popularity during the latter part of the nineteenth century (Smith, pp. 316–17).

41. *The Raccolta*, pp. 4–5.

42. Lambing, pp. 223–24, and *St. Vincent's Manual* [1854], pp. 491–92.

43. Herbert Thurston, "The Rosary," *The Month* 96 (Nov. 1900): 513, 620. Thurston found little evidence to connect the rosary with St. Dominic. While, according to George Shea, his view on this found wide favor among Catholic scholars, some, including Shea, have since argued for a tradition dating back to St. Dominic upon which Alan de Rupe drew (George W. Shea, "The Dominican Rosary," in *Mariology*, 3 vols., ed. Juniper B. Carol [Milwaukee: Bruce Pub. Co., 1961], 3:109–17).

44. See Garraghan, 2:96, and Wissel, 1:491.

45. *The Raccolta*, pp. 120–21.

46. Yrjo Hirn, *The Sacred Shrine: A Study of the Poetry and Art of the Catholic Church* (London: Faber and Faber, 1958), pp. 160–65.

47. *NCE*, s.v. "Immaculate Conception," by E. D. O'Connor.

48. *NCE*, s.v. "The Miraculous Medal," by J. I. Dirvin.

49. *CE*, s.v. "Heart of Mary, Devotion to," by Jean Bainvel, and John F. Murphy, "The Immaculate Heart," in Carol, 3:168–71.

50. *The Mission Book*, p. 109.

51. *St. Vincent's Manual* [1854], pp. 461–62. See also *The Mission Book*, p. 110.

52. Lambing, pp. 160–61, and Christian P. Ceroke, "The Scapular Devotion," in Carol, 3:134–35.

53. Ceroke, pp. 134–35.

54. See Benedict Zimmerman, "The Origin of the Scapular," *Irish Ecclesiastical Record* 9 (1901): 385–408 and 15 (1904): 142–53, 206–34, 331–51; Herbert Thurston, "The Origin of the Scapular: A Criticism," *Irish Ecclesiastical Record* 16 (1904): 59–75; idem, "Scapulars," *The Month* 149 (June 1927): 481–88 and 150 (July 1927): 44–58; Bartholomew F. M. Xiberta, *De Visione Sancti Simonis Stock* (Rome, 1950).

55. Thurston, "Scapulars," p. 56.

56. *The Golden Book of the Confraternities* (New York: Dunigan, 1854), pp. 128–29, and *St. Vincent's Manual* (rev. ed., Baltimore: Murphy, 1859), pp. 579–82.

57. Garraghan, 2:74–75, 82–84; Yuhaus, p. 250; and *The Mission Book*, pp. 109–12.

58. *CE*, s.v. "St. Joseph," by Charles L. Souvay.

59. *The Raccolta*, pp. 368–69.

60. Ibid., p. 442.

61. Ibid.

62. Marina Warner, *Alone of All Her Sex: The Myth and Cult of the Virgin Mary* (New York: Knopf, 1976), p. 283, and Herbert Thurston, "The Dedication of the Month of May to Our Lady," *The Month* 97 (May 1901):470.

63. *St. Vincent's Manual* [1854], p. 464.

64. Callahan, p. 40.

65. *The Raccolta*, pp. 328, 151, 164.

66. *The Raccolta*, pp. 264, 297, and *NCE*, s.v. "Novena," by P. K. Meagher.

67. Lambing, p. 195.

68. *The Raccolta*, p. 177.

69. See, e.g., *St. Vincent's Manual* and *The Golden Manual*, both of which contained numerous litanies.

70. *The Mission Book*, pp. 30–31. For similar instructions, see *The Ursuline Manual*, pp. 118–19; for an example of "devotions at Mass," see *St. Vincent's Manual* [1854], pp. 106–28, and *The Key of Heaven; or, A Manual of Prayer* (New York: O'Shea, 1873), pp. 134–207.

71. Callahan, pp. 337–38.

72. K. F. McMurtrie, "Liturgy and the Laity," *Orate Fratres* 3 (Oct. 6, 1929):414.

73. Louis Bouyer, *Liturgical Piety* (Notre Dame: University of Notre Dame Press, 1954), pp. 247–48.

74. "The Apostolate," *Orate Fratres* 12 (Mar. 20, 1938):224–25, and H. A. Reinhold, "Timely Tracts: A Long Question and a Short Answer," *Orate Fratres* 21 (June 15, 1947):368.

3. This World and the Other World

1. Peter Brown, *The Cult of the Saints: Its Rise and Function in Latin Christianity* (Chicago: University of Chicago Press, 1981), p. 61.

2. I[saac] T. Hecker, *The Church and the Age, an Exposition of*

the Catholic Church in View of the Needs and Aspirations of the Present Age (New York: Catholic Book Exchange, 1896), p. 260.

3. Faber, *All For Jesus; or, The Easy Ways of Divine Love* (23d Amer. ed., Baltimore: Murphy, 1854), pp. 128–29.

4. Orestes Brownson, *Saint-Worship/The Worship of Mary*, ed. Thomas R. Ryan (Patterson, N.J.: St. Anthony Guild Press, 1963), p. 74.

5. Ibid., pp. 74–75.

6. *Mirae caritatis*, May 28, 1902, quoted in *NCE*, s.v. "Communion of Saints," by F. X. Lawlor.

7. *CE*, s.v. "Communion of Saints," by F. J. Sollier.

8. Faber, *All For Jesus*, pp. 127–28.

9. Ibid.

10. Henry Charles Lea, *A History of Auricular Confession and Indulgences in the Latin Church*; vol. 3: *Indulgences* (Philadelphia: Lea Bros. & Co., 1896), pp. 25–26.

11. Ibid., 3:26.

12. "On Indulgences," *St. Vincent's Manual* [1854], pp. 536–37; see also Albert Michel, "La Communion des Saints," *Doctor Communis* 9 (1956):95–96.

13. On the differences between a gift and a money economy, see Natalie Zemon Davis, "The Gift in Sixteenth Century France," Ena Thompson Lecture Series, Pomona College, Oct. 1984.

14. *The Ursuline Manual*, pp. 116–17; slightly altered version of the same text in *St. Vincent's Manual* [1854], p. 102; similar instructions in *The Mission Book*, pp. 31, 37.

15. *The Catholic Manual* (Baltimore: F. Lucas, [1825?]), p. 155.

16. *The Mission Book*, p. 116.

17. *St. Vincent's Manual* [1854], p. 600.

18. Ibid., p. 431.

19. *The Ursuline Manual*, p. 570.

20. Ibid.

21. *The Mission Book*, p. 144.

22. *The Ursuline Manual*, p. 522.

23. "The Manner in Which We Celebrate the Feast of St. Joseph," *Ave Maria* (hereafter cited as *AM*) 9 (May 3, 1873):281.

24. *The Golden Book of the Confraternities*, p. 71.

25. *The Mission Book*, p. 109.

26. *The Ursuline Manual*, p. 117.

27. Paul R. Messbarger, *Fiction With a Parochial Purpose: Social*

Uses of American Catholic Literature, 1884–1900 (Boston: Boston University Press, 1971), p. 140.

28. *The Messenger of the Sacred Heart* (hereafter cited as *MSH*) 7 (Oct. 1872): 458–59. These ideas were still common enough to be parodied in the 1940s. Writing in *Orate Fratres*, H. A. Reinhold described "the good Father who has a special way of sanctification, just for you. Of course it is a special devotion. You just do *this* and it will do *that* for you. You say such and such a prayer, and wear such and such a thing, and send in this and that . . . and you will get whatever you want. His customers have acknowledged it, it is sure-fire. A soldier gets through battle safe (I quote), turkeys all survived, our house did not catch fire, father made his Easter duties, Bobby is better behaved, I got a baby of my own now — very sweet — I have a good position and got out of debt, somebody received the last sacraments, the kid got well, a terminal case of tuberculosis was healed, I won a lawsuit, my car was completely demolished in an accident but I survived to tell the tale — why did it not help the car too? — my pocketbook was found and returned, my boy-friend turned Catholic — all thanks to this one device" ("High-Pressure Salesmanship," *Orate Fratres* 28 [Nov. 28, 1943]: 33).

29. See, e.g., *AM* 15 (Aug. 16, 1879): 660; *AM* 15 (Apr. 5, 1879): 280–81; *AM* 8 (Sept. 7, 1872): 578–79.

30. *The Ave Maria Index* lists three full pages of entries under "Conversion" and more than four pages of entries under "Miracles," most of which were cures. (Some of the conversions and miracles were reprinted from other sources and some did not take place in the United States.) There are only a few entries under topics such as "Family" (3), "Mothers" (7), "Temperance" (5), "Young Men" (4), or even "Death" (12). See Mildred Florence Baumgartner, *The Ave Maria Index, Vol. 1–25: May 1865–December 1887* (Notre Dame: University of Notre Dame, n.d.).

31. J[ames] M[onroe] Buckley, *Faith-Healing, Christian Science and Kindred Phenomena* (New York: The Century Co., 1898), p. 38. On the growing emphasis on healing within Protestantism, see Raymond J. Cunningham, "From Holiness to Healing: The Faith Cure in America 1872–1892," *Church History* 43 (1974): 499–513.

32. [Rev. William Matthews], *A Collection of Affidavits and Certificates, relative to the wonderful cure of Mrs. Ann Mattingly, which took place in the City of Washington, D.C. on the tenth of March, 1824* (Washington: James Wilson, 1824); John England, *Examination of*

Evidence and Report to the Most Rev. James Whitfield, D.D., Archbishop of Baltimore upon the Miraculous Restoration of Mrs. Ann Mattingly of the City of Washington, D.C. Together with the Documents (Charleston, 1830); Bishop England's book was reprinted in *Ave Maria* 7 (May 6, 1871): 303ff., and the story of the cure was retold in Anna H. Dorsey, "The Old Gray Rosary," serialized in *AM* 3: 630ff. For information on Hohenlohe's intercessory activities on the continent, see Thomas A. Kselman, *Miracles and Prophecies in Nineteenth-Century France* (New Brunswick, N.J.: Rutgers University Press, 1983), pp. 23–24.

33. *Miracles, wrought by the intercession of Prince Hohenlohe, in the person of Miss Mary Lalor, of the Queen's County in Ireland, Miss Mary Stuart, of the city of Dublin, and Miss Barbary O'Connor, of England, with the pastoral letters of . . . Doctor Doyle, Roman Catholic Bishop of Kildare, and of Doctor Murray, Archbishop of Dublin . . .* (New York: James Costigan, 1823).

34. For a longer account of a cure attributed to the Sacred Heart of Jesus, see "Two Remarkable Favors," *MSH* 8 (June 1873): 274.

35. See, e.g., *AM* 15 (Aug. 16, 1879): 660; *AM* 15 (Apr. 5, 1879): 280–81; *AM* 8 (Sept. 7, 1872): 578–79.

36. See, e.g., "Another Remarkable Cure by the Water of Lourdes," *AM* 11 (Sept. 18, 1875): 613; "Miraculous Cure and Conversion by Means of the Water of Lourdes," *AM* 12 (Feb. 12, 1876): 107; "The Water of Lourdes," *AM* 9 (July 5, 1873): 426–27.

37. *Irish Faith in America: Recollections of a Missionary* (New York: Benziger Bros. [1881]), p. 61.

38. Ibid., pp. 62–63.

39. "Saved by a 'Hail Mary,'" *AM* 18 (Dec. 9, 1882): 974.

40. "The Scapular: An Incident of the Late War," *AM* 1 (July 15, 1865): 147.

41. Ibid., pp. 147–48.

42. Callahan, p. 107.

43. Ibid., p. 123. For other miracles associated with scapulars, see "Miracles Performed by Virtue of the Scapular," *The Golden Book of the Confraternities,* pp. 119–25.

44. "An Interesting Letter from Father Weninger, S.J.: Miraculous Cures Through the Intercession of Blessed Peter Claver," *AM* 22 (Mar. 13, 1886): 250–51; see also Garraghan, 2: 64.

45. "Miracles Wrought by Relics," reprinted from the New York *Sunday Mercury,* in *AM* 12 (June 17, 1876): 391–93; see also the New

York *Freeman's Journal*, Jan. 16 and 30, 1858; Yuhaus, pp. 263–68; and Dolan, *Catholic Revivalism*, pp. 145–46.

46. "A Cure at the Convent of Loretto," *AM* 2 (Dec. 22, 1866): 810–11.

47. Ibid.

48. "A Miraculous Cure in St. Louis," *AM* 3 (Oct. 12, 1867): 647–49.

49. Ibid.

50. Benedicta Ward, *Miracles and the Medieval Mind* (Philadelphia: University of Pennsylvania Press, 1983), p. 216.

51. "Last Moments of the Late Archbishop Spalding – His Devotion to the Blessed Virgin," *AM* 10 (July 25, 1874): 474–75.

52. *MSH* 2 (Sept. 1867): 348.

53. "The Scapular: An Incident of the Late War," *AM* 1 (July 15, 1865): 147.

54. "Saved by a 'Hail Mary,'" *AM* 18 (Dec. 9, 1882): 974.

55. "A Cure at the Convent of Loretto," *AM* 2 (Dec. 22, 1866): 811–12.

56. Bp. John Milner, *Authentic Documents Relative to the Miraculous Cure of Winefrid White, of Wolverhampton, at St. Winefrid's Well, alias,* HOLY-WELL, *in Flintshire, on the 28th day of June, 1805* (1st Amer. from the 3d London ed. Baltimore: B. Dornin, 1810), pp. 26–27.

57. Ibid., p. 35.

58. Ibid.

59. See James Monroe Buckley, *An Address on Supposed Miracles* (New York: Hurd and Houghton, 1875), for numerous examples of how a Protestant minister could explain away alleged miracles. For a more scholarly discussion of the theoretical difficulties involved in defining miracles, see Richard Swinburne, *The Concept of Miracle* (London: Macmillan & Co., 1970), pp. 1–10.

60. *MSH* 2 (Sept. 1867): 347.

61. Why they did not come to his notice was not explained. He may simply have meant that spiritual favors were less noticeable than temporal favors, and thus less often commented upon. But considering that people wrote in to describe the most ordinary events as temporal favors, it is more likely that more temporal favors came to the editor's attention because that is what his readers were watching for and writing in about.

62. Report of the "Confraternity of the Immaculate Conception," *AM* 15 (Apr. 5, 1879): 280–81.

63. "Miracles Wrought by Relics," reprinted from the New York *Sunday Mercury*, in *AM* 12 (June 17, 1876): 391.

64. "Miracles," *Freeman's Journal*, Jan. 30, 1858 (emphasis in the original).

65. McMaster states that the cures were miraculous "in the popular sense as extraordinary . . . but not in the sense that they could stand the test of the Sacred Congregation in Rome, for that is another question" (ibid).

66. "Miracles Wrought by Relics," p. 391.

67. "Miracles," *Freeman's Journal*, Jan. 30, 1858.

68. Ibid.

69. Yuhaus, p. 265.

70. "Miracles Wrought by Relics," pp. 392–93.

71. Ibid., pp. 391–92; Yuhaus, p. 265.

72. These two ways of perceiving miraculous cures parallel the "two social loops or cycles" identified by Tambiah in his study of Buddhist saints and their lay devotees. The first is ideologically developed and can be understood in terms of the Buddhist path of salvation; the second is "more hidden and manipulative and rides on the former." In the first instance, "amulets (like relics) act as *'reminders'* of the virtues of the saint and the Buddha," while in the second, lay people use "these amulets to influence, control, seduce, and exploit fellow laymen for worldly purposes" (Stanley Jeyaraja Tambiah, *The Buddhist Saints of the Forest and the Cult of Amulets* [Cambridge: Cambridge University Press, 1984], pp. 335–36).

4. THE AFFECTIVE BOND

1. Roger Aubert, *The Church in a Secularized Society* (New York: Paulist Press, 1978), p. 118.

2. Orestes Brownson, "Protestant Revivals and Catholic Retreats," *Brownson's Quarterly Review* 3 (July 1858): 292.

3. Ibid., p. 293.

4. See Wilfrid Parsons, *Early Catholic Americana: A List of Books and Other Works by Catholic Authors in the United States, 1729–1830* (New York: Macmillan, 1939) and CUA *Survey*.

5. The influence of *The Garden of the Soul* during the eighteenth and early nineteenth centuries was so great that the "old English" or hereditary Catholics were often referred to as "Garden-of-the-Soul Catholics" to distinguish them from "those [such as Faber] who en-

tered the Church at the time of the Oxford Movement, and whose devotions . . . were more fervid and expansive in expression" (Edwin H. Burton, *The Life and Times of Bishop Challoner, 1691–1781*, 2 vols. [New York and London: Longmans, Green and Co., 1909], 1:130–31).

6. Francis de Sales, *Introduction to a Devout Life* (New York: P. O'Shea, 1867), p. xv.

7. Ibid., p. 76.

8. Parsons and CUA *Survey.*

9. See John Sharp, "The Influence of St. Alphonsus Liguori in Nineteenth-Century Britain," *Downside Review* 101 (1983):61, for a discussion of Liguori's growing influence in England during the same period.

10. Their handbook summarized the content of the sermons to be preached at a mission, but directed the user to Liguori's works, specifically his *Sermons for Sunday* and *Preparation for Death*, for more extensive sketches (Wissel, 2:328–29). The sketches in *Preparation for Death*, as its subtitle indicates, could be used as either meditations or sermons.

11. Dolan refers to the choice of a life of piety as conversion and discusses it at length in *Catholic Revivalism.*

12. Although de Sales uses the terms "meditation" and "mental prayer" interchangeably, meditation or discursive prayer is only the most basic of the three methods of mental prayer: discursive, affective, and contemplative. See *NCE*, s.v. "Prayer," by K. J. Healy.

13. Ibid., p. 84.

14. Ibid., p. 85.

15. Ibid., p. 86.

16. Ibid.

17. Ibid., p. 88.

18. See Pierre Pourrat, *Christian Spirituality*, 4 vols. (vols. 1–3, London: Burns Oates & Washbourne, 1927; vol. 4, Westminster, Md.: Newman Press, 1955), 3:344–45.

19. Pourrat, 4:377.

20. Liguori, 3:276–80.

21. Ibid., 3:279 (emphasis added).

22. Ibid., 3:61.

23. Ibid., 6:125–26.

24. *The Mission Book*, p. 127.

25. Ibid., p. 128.

26. Ibid., p. 151.

27. Ibid., pp. 152–66.

28. Liguori, 3:269–70.

29. Ibid., 6:116.

30. Francis de Sales, p. 81.

31. Liguori, 6:264.

32. Ibid., 3:268.

33. Frederick W. Faber, *Growth in Holiness; or, the Progress of the Spiritual Life* (Baltimore: Murphy, n.d.), pp. 247–62.

34. Frederick W. Faber, *All For Jesus; or, the Easy Ways of Divine Love*, 23rd Amer. ed. (Baltimore: John Murphy, 1854), p. 66.

35. Frederick W. Faber, *The Foot of the Cross* (Baltimore: John Murphy, n.d.), p. 73.

36. Faber, *Growth in Holiness*, p. 405.

37. Frederick W. Faber, *Precious Blood; or, The Price of our Salvation*, 10th Amer. ed. (Baltimore: Murphy [1860]), p. 341.

38. Faber, *Growth in Holiness*, p. 405.

39. Ibid., p. 404.

40. Ibid., p. 7.

41. Ibid., pp. 218–19.

42. Melford E. Spiro, *Burmese Supernaturalism*, expanded ed. (Philadelphia: ISHI, 1978), pp. xxii, xxiv.

43. Ibid., p. xxv.

44. Ibid., p. xxvi.

45. *AM* 1 (Nov. 4, 1865):387–88.

46. "Last Moments of the Late Archbishop Spalding – His Devotion to the Blessed Virgin," *AM* 10 (July 25, 1874): p. 475.

47. *AM* 1 (Aug. 5, 1865):193.

48. "Legends of the Blessed Virgin," translated for *Ave Maria*, *AM* 1 (May 1, 1865):11 (emphasis added).

49. "The Power of the Pater and the Ave Maria," *AM* 1 (May 13, 1865):25.

50. "Great God! It is Jesus!" *AM* 1 (July 29, 1865):184.

51. "Leandro; or, the Sign of the Cross," *MSH* 4 (Feb. 1869):54–55.

52. Ibid., p. 55.

53. Nancy Chodorow, *The Reproduction of Mothering: Psychoanalysis and the Sociology of Gender* (Berkeley: University of California Press, 1978).

54. Although for the most part the sources discussed here do not provide enough detail to probe deep-structural meanings in anything

but the most general way, this account provides a classic illustration of the defensive use of a religious image.

Spiro, following Freud, assumes that all religious symbols function defensively on the deep-structural level. Recent work on object relations in psychoanalytic theory suggests that people's internal representations of parental figures may vary more widely across cultures than Freudian (drive) theory would predict. Moreover, evidence that an individual's internal representations of both parents and supernatural beings may change over time suggests that the way a person appropriates material from a given religious tradition may vary considerably over time. These developments in psychoanalytic theory raise the possibility that people may use religious symbols for transformative as well as defensive purposes. In light of this possibility specific deep-structural meanings need to be explored empirically and in context. See Ada-Maria Rizzuto, *The Birth of the Living God: A Psychoanalytic Study* (Chicago: University of Chicago Press, 1979); Ann Taves, "Magic, Metaphor, and Transitional Objects: Psychoanalytic Reflections on Women's Experience," paper presented at a conference on Feminism, Spirituality, and Wholeness sponsored by the Institute for Religion and Wholeness, Claremont, California, Apr. 18–20, 1985.

5. ORTHOPRAXIS AND ORTHODOXY

1. Marie-Hélène Froeschlé-Chopard, "Les Dévotions populaires d'après les visites pastorales: Un Example: le Diocèse de Vence au début du XVIIIe siècle," *Revue d'histoire de l'église de France* 60 (1974): 85–86.

2. Ibid., p. 99.

3. Ibid., p. 90.

4. Ibid., p. 99.

5. Ibid.

6. Marie-Hélène Froeschlé-Chopard, "The Iconography of the Sacred Universe in the Eighteenth Century: Chapels and Churches in the Diocese of Vence and Grasse," in *Ritual, Religion, and the Sacred: Selections from the Annales*, vol. 7, ed. Robert Forster and Orest Ranum (Baltimore and London: Johns Hopkins University Press, 1982), p. 173.

7. Froeschlé-Chopard, "Dévotions," p. 89.

8. Ibid. *Ainsi, ces cultes ne sont qu'apparemment reçus, apparem-*

*ment orthodoxes: ils ont, au niveau populaire, une toute autre significa-
tion que celle qui est explicitement donnée par la doctrine.*

9. William A. Christian, Jr., *Person and God in a Spanish Valley*
(New York and London: Seminar Press, 1972), pp. 181–82.

10. Ibid., p. 181.

11. Ibid.

12. William A. Christian, Jr., *Local Religion in Sixteenth-Century
Spain* (Princeton: Princeton University Press, 1981), p. 179.

13. John Bossy, "The Counter-Reformation and the People of
Catholic Europe," *Past and Present* 47 (May 1970):53.

14. Ibid., p. 52.

15. Richard W. Southern, *Western Society and the Church in the
Middle Ages* (New York: Penquin Books, 1970), pp. 136–37.

16. Ibid., pp. 138–39.

17. Henry Charles Lea, *A History of Auricular Confession and Indulgences in the Latin Church;* vol. 3: *Indulgences* (Philadelphia: Lea
Bros. & Co., 1896), p. 9.

18. Ibid.

19. Ronald Finucane, *Miracles and Pilgrims: Popular Beliefs in Medieval England* (Totowa, N.J.: Rowman and Littlefield, 1977), pp.
44–45.

20. Lea, 3:528.

21. *NCE* s.v. "Indulgences, Apostolic," by O. A. Boenki; Lea, 3:
509.

22. *The Raccolta*, p. xix.

23. Ibid., p. xxiii.

24. Lionel Rothkrug, "Popular Religion and Holy Shrines: Their
Influence on the Origins of the German Reformation and Their Role
in German Cultural Development," in *Religion and the People, 800–
1700*, ed. James Obelkevich (Chapel Hill: University of North Carolina Press, 1979), p. 34, and Bossy, "Counter-Reformation," p. 59.

25. Bossy, ibid.

26. Lea, 3:475.

27. Timothy Tackett, *Priest and Parish in Eighteenth-Century
France: A Social and Political Study of the Curés in a Diocese of Dauphiné* (Princeton: Princeton University Press, 1977), pp. 196–97.

28. Ibid., p. 198.

29. Ibid., p. 199.

30. Ibid., p. 200.

31. Ibid., pp. 199–200.

32. Ibid., p. 201.

33. See Tackett, chap. 10; Bossy, "Counter-Reformation," p. 60; Thomas Kselman, *Miracles and Prophecies in Nineteenth-Century France* (Rutgers, N.J.: Rutgers University Press, 1983), p. 166.

34. See Emmet Larkin, "The Devotional Revolution in Ireland," *American Historical Review* 77 (June 1972):645; Lynn Hollen Lees, *Exiles of Erin: Irish Migrants in Victorian London* (Ithaca, N.Y.: Cornell University Press, 1979), pp. 177–79; Sheridan Gilley, "Catholic Faith of the Irish Slums, London, 1840–70," in *The Victorian City: Images and Realities*, ed. H. J. Dyos and Michael Wolf (London and Boston: Routledge and Kegan Paul, 1973), pp. 846–48.

35. Lea, 3:481.

36. Guilday, pp. 212–13.

37. Kselman, p. 166.

38. Although the Apostolate of Prayer was not technically a confraternity, it was similar in structure to the other two organizations.

39. Kselman, pp. 35–36.

40. Ibid., p. 168.

41. Ralph L. and Henry F. Woods, *Pilgrim Places in North America* (New York and Toronto: Longmans, Green & Co., 1939). The Woodses' guide to Catholic shrines was the first, and as far as I know only, attempt to describe Catholic shrines in the United States. The Woodses define "shrines" broadly to include "all those places in America having an appeal . . . that is wider [than] . . . the appeal of the local church" (pp. xi–xii). To come up with the eleven shrines, I excluded shrines in Mexico, Canada, and areas of the United States colonized by Spain (Florida and the Southwest) as well as shrines for which no founding date was given. The shrines and their locations are as follows: Shrine of Our Lady of Prompt Succor, Ursuline Convent, New Orleans, pp. 58–62; The Sorrowful Mother, Congregation of the Precious Blood, Frank, Ohio, pp. 129–30; Chapel Shrine of the Immaculate Conception, Robinsonville, Wisc., pp. 153–56; Holy Cross Grotto of Lourdes, parish church, Cincinnati, Ohio, pp. 123–24; Shrine of St. John Berchmans, Sacred Heart Convent, Grand Coteau, La., pp. 54–56; St. Roch's Campo Santo and Shrine, New Orleans, pp. 57–58; Shrine of Our Lady of Perpetual Help, Redemptorists (church), Boston, pp. 70–71; Shrine of Holy Relics, Convent of the Sisters of the Precious Blood, Maria Stein, Ohio, pp. 130–32; St. Ann's Shrine, parish church (French Canadian), Fall River, Mass., pp. 71–72; Shrine of Our Lady of Lourdes, Fathers of Mercy (church), New

York City, pp. 101–02; and Our Lady of Consolation Shrine, Carey, Ohio, p. 122.

42. "Shrines of the Blessed Virgin," *AM* 8 (Jan. 13, 1872): 17.

43. "Review of *Mater Admirabilis; or, First Fifteen Years of Mary Immaculate* by Rev. Alfred Monnin," *Catholic World* 1 (June 1865): 430.

44. Ibid.

45. Ibid., p. 431.

46. Ibid., pp. 154–55. For an account of another Marian apparition to a lay woman in Wisconsin exactly 92 years later which also met with ecclesiastical disapproval, see Thomas A. Kselman, "Our Lady of Necedah: Marian Piety and the Cold War," Cushwa Center (University of Notre Dame), *Working Paper Series* 12/2 (Fall 1982).

47. Froeschlé-Chopard, "Dévotions," p. 99; idem, "Iconography," p. 173; Christian, *People and God*, p. 183.

48. Orestes Brownson, "The Miracles of the Saints," *AM* 2 (May 26, 1866): 328–29.

49. Peter Brown, "Society and the Supernatural: A Medieval Change," *Daedalus* 104 (1975): 144.

50. Ibid.

51. Frederick W. Faber, *Devotion to the Pope* (Baltimore: John Murphy, 1860), pp. 9–10.

52. Ibid., pp. 12–13.

53. Ibid., p. 19.

54. Ibid., pp. 19–20.

55. Ibid., p. 23.

56. Ibid., pp. 31–32.

57. Ibid., p. 30.

58. Faber, *Growth in Holiness*, p. 274.

59. Most discussions of Pius IX's definition of the Immaculate Conception follow Msgr. Talbot, a nineteenth-century English bishop, in stressing that the manner in which the doctrine was defined was more important than the doctrine itself. They thus stress its importance as a practical and precedent-setting manifestation of papal infallibility. See, e.g., Derek Holmes, *The Triumph of the Holy See: A Short History of the Papacy in the Nineteenth Century* (Shepherdstown, W. Va.: Patmos Press, 1978), p. 142. But as William McSweeney points out, "there are less contentious beliefs which the Pope might have chosen as a vehicle for promoting his infallibility had his enthusiasm

for the Virgin Mary been secondary, as Talbot implies" (William Mc-
Sweeney, *Roman Catholicism: The Search for Relevance* [New York:
St. Martin's Press, 1980], p. 43).

60. Paul Ricoeur, *The Symbolism of Evil* (Boston: Beacon Press,
1967), p. 35.

61. Ibid., p. 29.

62. Ibid., pp. 28–29.

63. Benedictine Monks of Solesmes, eds., *Papal Teachings, Our
Lady* (Boston: Daughters of St. Paul, 1961), pp. 61–62.

64. Ibid., p. 71.

65. Ibid., p. 74.

66. Mary Douglas, *Purity and Danger: An Analysis of the Concepts of Pollution and Taboo* (London and Henley: Routledge and Kegan
Paul, 1966), p. 115.

67. Monks of Solesmes, p. 63.

68. Gerhard Ebeling, *The Word of God and Tradition: Historical
Studies Interpreting the Divisions of Christianity* (London: Wm. Collins Sons & Co., 1968), p. 187.

69. Ibid.

70. A. Gratry, *The Month of Mary Conceived Without Sin*, trans.
and intro. by F. W. Faber (Baltimore: Kelly, Hedian and Piet, 1861),
p. ix.

71. Monks of Solesmes, p. 81.

72. Ibid., pp. 81, 83.

73. Gratry, p. ix–xi.

74. Pastoral letter of Archbishop James Roosevelt Bayley on the
occasion of the consecration of the Archdiocese of Baltimore to the
Sacred Heart, printed in *MSH* 8 (Nov. 1873):495.

75. Ibid.

6. Devotions in the American Context

1. Thomas T. McAvoy, "The Formation of the Catholic Minority in the United States, 1820–1860," *Review of Politics* 10 (1948):26.

2. Ibid., p. 34.

3. Ibid., p. 14.

4. William V. Shannon, *The American Irish*, rev. ed. (New York:
Macmillan Co., 1966), pp. 19–20, 25.

5. These studies are cited below.

6. Holmes, *The Triumph of the Holy See*, p. 135. For a general

discussion of the Romanization of devotion during the pontificate of Pius IX, see also Aubert, pp. 117–24.

7. Lingard to Walker, 1850, quoted in Chinnici, *The English Catholic Enlightenment: John Lingard and the Cisalpine Movement, 1780–1850* (Shepherdstown, W. Va.: Patmos Press, 1980), pp. 147–48.

8. Orestes Brownson, "Capes's Four Years' Experience," *Brownson's Quarterly Review* (July 1850), in Brownson's *Works* 20:21–22.

9. For background on the group, see Robert Emmett Curran, "Prelude to 'Americanism': The New York Accademia and Clerical Radicalism in the Late Nineteenth Century," *Church History* 47 (Mar. 1978):48–65. Curran says very little about their attitude toward devotional practices, however. For a brief description of liberal Catholic attitudes toward devotionalism in the eighties and nineties, see Robert D. Cross, *The Emergence of Liberal Catholicism in America* (Cambridge: Harvard University Press, 1958), pp. 165–66.

10. James Hennesey, *American Catholics: A History of the Roman Catholic Community in the United States* (New York: Oxford University Press, 1981), p. 167.

11. Callahan, p. 78.

12. Ibid., p. 107.

13. Ibid., p. 100.

14. Burtsell referred in his diary to an essay that he had written on liturgical languages; he related that he had given it "to Frs. Hecker and Young who approved of it: and wish it to be published in the Catholic World: in such a tone as to be a wedge for the change of language in the liturgy: though now only asking for the adoption of the vernacular in voluntary devotions" (p. 349). See also Curran, p. 53.

15. Martin Kirk, "The Spirituality of Isaac Thomas Hecker Reconciling the American Character and the Catholic Faith" (Ph.D. dissertation, St. Louis University, 1980), pp. 238–40.

16. Callahan, pp. 334, xviii.

17. Ibid., pp. 409–10.

18. James Hennesey, "Papacy and Episcopacy in Nineteenth Century American Catholic Thought," *Records of the American Catholic Historical Society of Philadelphia* 77 (1966):176.

19. See Derek Holmes, *More Roman than Rome: English Catholicism in the Nineteenth Century* (Shepherdstown, W. Va.: Patmos Press, 1978) on Manning, and Emmet Larkin, "The Devotional Revolution in Ireland" on Cullen.

20. Joseph P. Chinnici, "Organization of the Spiritual Life: American Catholic Devotional Works, 1791–1866," *Theological Studies* 40 (June 1979): 233–34.

21. *Acta et decreta sacrorum conciliorum recentiorum collectio lacensis* 3, p. 502, quoted in Chinnici, p. 234.

22. See Kerr, p. 137; Connolly, pp. 264–78; David W. Miller, "Irish Catholicism and the Great Famine," *Journal of Social History* 9 (1975): 87; Emmet Larkin, "The Devotional Revolution in Ireland," p. 649; Desmond Fennell, "The Myth of the Irish: A Failure of American Catholic Scholarship," in his *The Changing Face of Catholic Ireland* (London: Geoffrey Chapman, 1968), p. 123; Dennis J. Clark, "The Irish Catholics: A Postponed Perspective," in *Immigrants and Religion in Urban America*, ed. Randall M. Miller and Thomas D. Marzik (Philadelphia: Temple University Press, 1977), pp. 53, 56–57.

23. Shannon, p. 21.

24. Larkin, p. 649.

25. Fennell, p. 123.

26. Larkin, p. 649.

27. See Lees, pp. 193–97, for a discussion of Roman Catholicism and Irish identity in mid-nineteenth-century London that makes a similar point.

28. Thomas H. Burke, O. P., "The Supernatural Life of the Irish People," in *Lectures on Faith and Fatherland* (London: n.d.), p. 117, quoted in Larkin, p. 649.

29. Dale Beryl Light, Jr., "Class, Ethnicity, and Urban Ecology in a Nineteenth Century City: Philadelphia's Irish, 1840–1890" (Ph.D. dissertation, University of Pennsylvania, 1979), p. 94.

30. Thomas N. Brown, "The Origins and Character of Irish Nationalism," *Review of Politics* 18 (1956): 346–47.

31. Ibid.

32. Ellen Skerrett, "The Irish Parish in Chicago, 1880–1930," Cushwa Center (University of Notre Dame), *Working Paper Series* 9/2 (Spring 1981): 8.

33. Mulkerins, *Holy Family Parish*, pp. 124–25, and Garraghan, 2: 202.

34. Mulkerins, p. 18.

35. Ibid., p. 20.

36. Ibid.

37. Ibid., p. 23.

38. Ibid., pp. 17–23.

39. Ibid., p. 26.

40. Ibid., pp. 283–84.

41. Ibid., p. 285.

42. Ibid., p. 300.

43. Ibid., p. 288.

44. Ibid., p. 299.

45. Ibid., p. 289.

46. Ibid., p. 305.

47. St. Joseph was the patron saint of the church until Pope Leo XIII designated a feast day for the Holy Family.

48. Mulkerins, pp. 37, 38, 107.

49. Ibid., p. 39.

50. Ibid., p. 52.

51. Ibid., pp. 38–44, 52.

52. Ibid., p. 931 (emphasis added).

53. Msgr. d'Hulst, quoted in Aubert, p. 132.

54. For a discussion of the role of ethnic organizations and institutions in the creation of a subculture, see Milton Gordon, *Assimilation in American Life: The Role of Race, Religion and National Origins* (New York: Oxford University Press, 1964). Studies of the Irish in nineteenth-century American cities frequently comment on the role of the church and its associations in the creation of an enclosed immigrant subculture. See, e.g., Earl F. Niehaus, *The Irish in New Orleans, 1800–1860* (Baton Rouge: Louisiana State University Press, 1965), p. 98; Dennis Clark, *The Irish in Philadelphia: Ten Generations of Urban Experience* (Philadelphia: Temple University Press, 1973), p. 99; Patricia K. Good, "Irish Adjustment to American Society: Integration or Separation? A Portrait of an Irish-Catholic Parish: 1863–1886," *Records of the American Catholic Historical Society* 86 (1975): 13–14; Edward Kantowicz, "Church and Neighborhood," *Ethnicity* 7 (1980): 355–56; Kathleen Gavigan, "The Rise and Fall of Parish Cohesiveness in Philadelphia," *Records of the American Catholic Historical Society* 86 (1975): 111–12; Stephan Thernstrom, *Poverty and Progress: Social Mobility in a Nineteenth Century City* (Cambridge: Harvard University Press, 1964), p. 179.

55. Peter Berger, *The Sacred Canopy: Elements of a Sociological Theory of Religion* (Garden City, N.Y.: Doubleday & Co., 1967; Anchor Books, 1969), p. 138.

56. On Catholic missions as analogs of Protestant revivals, see Jay Dolan, *Catholic Revivalism*, pp. 187–92.

57. William G. McLoughlin, Jr., *Modern Revivalism: Charles Grandison Finney to Billy Graham* (New York: Ronald Press, 1959).

58. Sandra J. Sizer, *Gospel Hymns and Social Religion: The Rhetoric of Nineteenth-Century Revivalism* (Philadelphia: Temple University Press, 1978).

59. William Haller, *The Elect Nation: The Meaning and Relevance of Foxe's Book of Martyrs* (New York: Harper and Row, 1963), p. 52, quoted in Eisenstein, 1:421 (emphasis added).

60. Gerald P. Fogarty, "The Quest for a Catholic Vernacular Bible in America," in *The Bible in America: Essays in Cultural History*, ed. Nathan O. Hatch and Mark A. Noll (New York and Oxford: Oxford University Press, 1982), p. 177.

61. Eisenstein, 1:424–25, and Colleen McDannell, "Victorian Domestic Architecture and the Transformation of American Protestantism," unpublished paper delivered at the annual meeting of the American Academy of Religion, December 1982.

62. Hugh McLeod, *Religion and the People of Western Europe, 1789–1970* (Oxford and New York: Oxford University Press, 1981), p. 36.

63. Sizer, p. 157.

64. David Brion Davis, "Some Themes of Counter-Subversion: An Analysis of Anti-Masonic, Anti-Catholic, and Anti-Mormon Literature," *Mississippi Valley Historical Review* 47 (Sept. 1960):214.

65. Ibid., p. 215.

66. Martin E. Marty, "The Catholic Ghetto and All the Other Ghettos," *Catholic Historical Review* 68 (Apr. 1982):188 (emphasis added).

67. Edwin Scott Gaustad, *Historical Atlas of Religion in America* (New York: Harper and Row, 1962), figure 95, p. 110.

68. Timothy L. Smith, "Protestant Schooling and American Nationality, 1800–1850," *Journal of American History* 53 (March 1967):680. See also Soltow and Stevens, p. 89.

69. Robert Francis Hueston, *The Catholic Press and Nativism, 1840–1860* (New York: Arno Press, 1976), pp. 52, 168.

70. Fogarty, pp. 163–66, and Hueston, p. 71.

71. Hueston, p. 327 (emphasis added).

72. Kaestle, pp. 169–70.

73. *AM* 1 (May 1, 1865):2–3.

74. Ibid.

75. Ibid.

76. Ibid.

Bibliography

PRIMARY SOURCES

Periodicals

Ave Maria
Brownson's Quarterly Review
The Catholic World
The Freeman's Journal
The Messenger of the Sacred Heart

Books

Benedictine Monks of Solesmes, eds. *Papal Teachings, Our Lady.* Boston: Daughters of St. Paul, 1961.

Brownson, Orestes. *Saint Worship/The Worship of Mary.* Edited and abridged by Thomas R. Ryan. Patterson, N.J.: St. Anthony Guild Press, 1963.

————. *The Works of Orestes A. Brownson.* 20 vols. Edited by Henry Brownson. Detroit: Thorndike Nourse, 1882–1887.

Buckley, James Monroe. *An Address on Supposed Miracles. Delivered Monday, September 20, 1875, before the New York ministers' meeting of the Methodist Episcopal church.* New York: Hurd and Houghton, 1875.

————. *Faith-Healing, Christian Science, and Kindred Phenomena.* New York: The Century Co., 1898.

Callahan, Thomas J., ed. *The Diary of Richard Burtsell, Priest of New York: The Early Years, 1865–1868.* New York: Arno Press, 1978.

The Catholic Manual. Baltimore: F. Lucas [1825].

Deshon, George. *Guide for Catholic Young Women.* 29th rev. ed. New

York: Catholic Book Exchange, 1897; reprint ed., New York: Arno Press, 1978.

England, John, Bishop. *Examination of Evidence and Report to the Most Rev. James Whitfield, D.D., Archbishop of Baltimore, Upon the Miraculous Restoration of Mrs. Ann Mattingly of the City of Washington, D. C. Together with the Documents.* Charleston: Burges, 1830.

Faber, Frederick W. *All For Jesus; or, The Easy Ways of Divine Love.* 23d Amer. ed. Baltimore: John Murphy, 1854.

———. *Devotion to the Pope.* Baltimore: John Murphy, 1860.

———. *The Foot of the Cross; or, The Sorrows of Mary.* Baltimore: John Murphy, n.d.

———. *Growth in Holiness; or, The Progress of the Spiritual Life.* Baltimore: John Murphy, n.d.

———. *The Precious Blood; or, The Price of Our Salvation.* 10th Amer. ed. Baltimore: John Murphy [1860].

Fitton, James, ed. *St. Joseph's Manual.* Boston: Noonan, 1877.

Francis of Sales. *Introduction to a Devout Life.* New York: P. O'Shea, 1867.

The Golden Book of the Confraternities. New York: Dunigan, 1854.

Gratry, A. *The Month of Mary Conceived Without Sin.* Translated and introduced by F. W. Faber. Baltimore: Kelly, Hedian and Piet, 1861.

Hay, George, Bishop. *The Scripture Doctrine of Miracles Displayed: in which their nature, etc., are impartially examined and explained, according to the light of revelation and the principles of sound reason.* New York: Dunigan, 1851.

Hecker, I[saac] T. *Aspirations of the Soul.* 3d ed. New York: James B. Kirker, 1959.

———. *The Church and the Age: An Exposition of the Catholic Church in View of the Needs and Aspirations of the Present Age.* New York: Catholic Book Exchange, 1896.

Irish Faith in America: Recollections of a Missionary. Translated by Ella McMahon. New York: Benziger Bros. [1881].

Liguori, Alphonsus. *The Complete Works of Saint Alphonsus de Liguori.* Edited by Eugene Grimm. The Ascetical Works, vol. 1: *Preparation for Death; or, Considerations on the Eternal Truths, Useful to All as Meditations and Serviceable to Priests for Sermons.* 2d ed. New York: Benziger Bros., 1887.

———. *The Complete Works of Saint Alphonsus de Liguori.* Edited by Eugene Grimm. The Ascetical Works, vol. 3: *The Great Means of Salvation and Perfection.* 2d ed. New York: Benziger Bros., 1887.

————. *The Complete Works of Saint Alphonsus de Liguori.* Edited by Eugene Grimm. The Ascetical Works, vol. 6: *The Holy Eucharist.* 2d ed. New York: Benziger Bros., 1887.

————. *Complete Ascetical Works of St. Alphonsus Liguori.* Edited by Eugene Grimm. Vol. 6: *The Holy Eucharist.* 3d ed. Brooklyn: Redemptorist Fathers, 1934.

[————]. *The Mission Book of the Congregation of the Most Holy Redeemer.* Baltimore: Kelly & Piet, 1862; reprint ed., New York: Arno Press, 1978.

A Manual of Catholic Devotions. Baltimore: John Murphy, 1859.

Manual of the Children of Mary. New York: P. J. Kenedy & Sons, 1878.

[Matthews, William, Rev.] *A Collection of Affidavits and Certificates, Relative to the Wonderful Cure of Mrs. Ann Mattingly, Which Took Place in the City of Washington, D. C. on the Tenth of March, 1824.* Washington, D. C.: James Wilson, 1824.

Middleton, Conyers. *A Free Inquiry into the Miraculous Powers, which are supposed to have subsisted in the Christian church, from the earliest ages through several successive centuries. By which it is shewn, that we have no sufficient reason to believe, upon the authority of the primitive fathers, that any such powers were continued to the church, after the days of the apostles.* London: Printed for R. Manby & H. S. Cox, 1749.

Milner, John, Bishop. *Authentic Documents Relative to the Miraculous Cure of Winefrid White, of Wolverhampton, at St. Winefrid's Well, alias, Holy-well, in Flintshire, on the 28th day of June, 1805.* 1st Amer. from the 3d London ed. Baltimore: Bernard Dornin, 1810.

Miracles, Wrought by the Intercession of Prince Hohenlohe, in the Person of Miss Mary Lalor, of the Queen's County in Ireland, Miss Mary Stuart, of the city of Dublin, and Miss Barbary O'Connor, of England, with the Pastoral Letters of . . . Doctor Doyle, Roman Catholic Bishop of Kildare, and Doctor Murray, Archbishop of Dublin. New York: James Costigan, 1823.

Newman, John Henry, *Two Essays on Biblical and on Ecclesiastical Miracles.* 7th ed. London and New York: Longmans, Green and Co., 1888.

The Raccolta; or, Collection of Prayers and Good Works to Which the Sovereign Pontiffs have attached Holy Indulgences. Published by Order of His Holiness, Pope Pius IX. Translated, authorized, and approved by the Sacred Congregation of Holy Indulgences. Woodstock, Md.: Woodstock College, 1878.

St. Vincent's Manual. Baltimore: John Murphy, 1854.

Spalding, M[artin] J. *Sketches of the Early Catholic Missions of Kentucky; From Their Commencement in 1787, to the Jubilee of 1826–7.* Louisville: B. J. Webb & Bro., 1844; reprint ed., New York: Arno Press, 1972.

The Ursuline Manual. New York: Dunigan, 1857.

Wissel, Joseph. *The Redemptorist on the American Missions.* 3 vols. 3d ed. Privately printed, 1920; reprint ed., New York: Arno Press, 1978.

SECONDARY SOURCES

Spirituality and Popular Devotions

"The Apostolate." *Orate Fratres* 12 (March 20, 1938): 224–25.

Attwater, Donald, ed. *A Catholic Dictionary.* 3d ed. New York: Macmillan Co., 1961. S.v. "Devotions, Popular"; "Liturgical Worship"; and "Liturgy."

Broderick, Robert C., ed. *The Catholic Encyclopedia.* Nashville: Thomas Nelson, 1976. S.v. "Paraliturgical Actions."

Bouyer, Louis. *Liturgical Piety.* Notre Dame: University of Notre Dame Press, 1955.

Brauer, Jerald C. "Conversion: From Puritanism to Revivalism." *The Journal of Religion* 58 (1978): 227–43.

Brown, Peter. *The Cult of the Saints: Its Rise and Function in Late Antiquity.* Chicago: University of Chicago Press, 1981.

The Catholic Encyclopedia. S.v. "Communion of Saints," by F. J. Sollier; "Heart of Jesus, Devotion to," by Jean Bainvel; "St. Joseph," by Charles L. Souvay; "Visits to the Blessed Sacrament," by Herbert Thurston.

Ceroke, Christian P. "The Scapular Devotion." In *Mariology,* 3 vols., 3: 128–42. Edited by Juniper B. Carol. Milwaukee: Bruce Publishing Co., 1961.

Chinnici, Joseph P. "The Organization of the Spiritual Life: American Catholic Devotional Works, 1791–1866." *Theological Studies* 40 (June 1979): 229–55.

Christian, William A., Jr. *Local Religion in Sixteenth-Century Spain.* Princeton: Princeton University Press, 1981.

————. *Person and God in a Spanish Valley*. New York and London: Seminar Press, 1972.

Connolly, Sean J. *Priests and People in Pre-Famine Ireland, 1780–1845*. New York: St. Martin's Press, 1982.

Cunningham, Raymond. "From Holiness to Healing: The Faith Cure in America 1872–1892." *Church History* 43 (1974): 499–513.

Danaher, Kevin, *The Year in Ireland: A Calendar*. Cork: Mercier Press, 1972.

Dehne, Carl. "Roman Catholic Popular Devotions." *Worship* 49 (1975): 446–60.

Dolan, Jay P. *Catholic Revivalism: The American Experience, 1830–1900*. Notre Dame: University of Notre Dame Press, 1978.

Dompnier, Bernard. "Un Aspect de la dévotion eucharistique dans la France du XVIIᵉ siècle: Les Prières des Quarante-Heures." *Revue d'histoire de l'église de France* 67 (1981): 5–31.

Finucane, Ronald. *Miracles and Pilgrims: Popular Beliefs in Medieval England*. Totowa, N.J.: Rowman and Littlefield, 1977.

Fish, Lydia Marie. "Roman Catholicism as Folk Religion in Buffalo." *Indiana Folklore* 9 (1976): 165–74.

Froeschlé-Chopard, Marie-Hélène. "Les Dévotions populaires d'après les visites pastorales: Un Example: Le Diocése de Vence au début du XVIIIᵉ siècle." *Revue d'histoire de l'église de France* 60 (1974): 85–100.

————. "The Iconography of the Sacred Universe in the Eighteenth Century: Chapels and Churches in the Diocese of Vence and Grasse." In *Ritual, Religion, and the Sacred: Selections from the Annales*, Vol. 7, pp. 146–81. Edited by Robert Forster and Orest Ranum. Translated by Elborg Forster and Orest Ranum. Baltimore and London: Johns Hopkins University Press, 1982.

Gilley, Sheridan. "Catholic Faith of the Irish Slums, London, 1840–70." In *The Victorian City*, pp. 834–53. Edited by H. J. Dyos and Michael Wolf. London and Boston: Routledge and Kegan Paul, 1973.

Guibert, Joseph de. *The Jesuits: Their Spiritual Doctrine and Practice; A Historical Study*. Translated by William J. Young. Edited by George E. Ganss. Chicago: Institute of Jesuit Sources, 1964.

Hambrick-Stowe, Charles E. *The Practice of Piety: Puritan Devotional Disciplines in Seventeenth-Century New England*. Chapel Hill: University of North Carolina Press, 1982.

Hirn, Yrjo. *The Sacred Shrine: A Study of the Poetry and Art of the Catholic Church*. London: Faber and Faber, 1958.

Kerr, Donal. "The Early Nineteenth Century: Patterns of Change" [in Irish Spirituality]. In *Irish Spirituality*, pp. 135–44. Edited by Michael Maher. Dublin: Veritas Publications, 1981.

Kirk, Martin. "The Spirituality of Isaac Thomas Hecker Reconciling the American Character and the Catholic Faith." Ph.D. dissertation, St. Louis University, 1980.

Kselman, Thomas A. *Miracles and Prophecies in Nineteenth-Century France*. New Brunswick, N.J.: Rutgers University Press, 1983.

————. "Our Lady of Necedah: Marian Piety and the Cold War." Cushwa Center (University of Notre Dame), *Working Paper Series* 12 (1982).

Lambing, Andrew Arnold. *The Sacramentals of the Holy Catholic Church*. 2d ed. New York: Benziger Bros., 1896.

Larkin, Emmet. "The Devotional Revolution in Ireland." *American Historical Review* 77 (1972): 625–52.

Lea, Henry Charles. *A History of Auricular Confession and Indulgences in the Latin Church*. Vol. 3: *Indulgences*. Philadelphia: Lea Bros. and Co., 1896.

LeBrun, Jacques. "Politics and Spirituality: The Devotion to the Sacred Heart." Translated by J. Griffiths. In *The Concrete Christian Life*, pp. 29–43. Edited by Christian Duquoc. New York: Herder and Herder, 1971.

McMurtrie, K. F. "Liturgy and the Laity." *Orate Fratres* 3 (October 6, 1929): 414–20.

Mentag, John V. "Catholic Spiritual Revivals: Parish Missions in the Midwest to 1865." Ph.D. dissertation, Loyola University, 1957.

Michel, Albert. "La Communion des Saints." *Doctor Communis* 9 (1956): 1–130.

Pochin Mould, Daphne D. C. *Irish Pilgrimage*. New York: The Devin-Adair Co., 1957.

Murphy, John F. "The Immaculate Heart." In *Mariology*, 3 vols., 3: 168–78. Edited by Juniper B. Carol. Milwaukee: Bruce Publishing Co., 1961.

The New Catholic Encyclopedia. S.v. "Benediction of the Blessed Sacrament," by M. Burbach; "Communion of Saints," by F. X. Lawlor; "Immaculate Conception," by E. D. O'Connor; "The Miraculous Medal," by J. I. Dirvin; "Novena," by P. K. Meagher; and "Prayer," by K. J. Healy.

Pourrat, Pierre, *Christian Spirituality*, 4 vols. Vols. 1–3, London: Burns Oates and Washbourne, 1927; Vol. 4, Westminster, Md.: Newman Press, 1955.

Reinhold, H. A. *The American Parish and the Roman Liturgy: An Essay in Seven Chapters*. New York: Macmillan, 1958.

————. "Timely Tracts: A Long Question and a Short Answer." *Orate Fratres* 21 (June 15, 1947): 363–69.

Rothkrug, Lionel. "Popular Religion and Holy Shrines: Their Influence on the Origins of the German Reformation and Their Role in German Cultural Development." In *Religion and the People, 800–1700*, pp. 20–86. Edited by James Obelkevich. Chapel Hill: University of North Carolina Press, 1979.

Shea, George W. "The Dominican Rosary." In *Mariology*, 3 vols., 3: 88–127. Edited by Juniper B. Carol. Milwaukee: Bruce Publishing Co., 1961.

Sizer, Sandra J. *Gospel Hymns and Social Religion: The Rhetoric of Nineteenth-Century Revivalism*. Philadelphia: Temple University Press, 1978.

Stierli, Josef. "The Development of the Church's Devotion to the Sacred Heart in Modern Times." In *The Heart of the Saviour: A Symposium on Devotion to the Sacred Heart*, pp. 59–107. Edited by Josef Stierli. New York: Herder and Herder, 1958.

————. "Devotion to the Sacred Heart From the End of Patristic Times Down to St. Margaret Mary." In *The Heart of the Saviour: A Symposium on Devotion to the Sacred Heart*, pp. 59–107. Edited by Josef Stierli. New York: Herder and Herder, 1958.

Tackett, Timothy. *Priest and Parish in Eighteenth-Century France: A Social and Political Study of the Curés in a Diocese of Dauphiné*. Princeton: Princeton University Press, 1977.

Tambiah, Stanley Jeyaraja. *The Buddhist Saints of the Forest and the Cult of Amulets*. Cambridge: Cambridge University Press, 1984.

Thurston, Herbert. "The Benediction of the Blessed Sacrament." *The Month* 97 (1901): 587–97, and 98 (1901): 58–69, 186–93, 264–76.

————. "The Dedication of the Month of May to Our Lady." *The Month* 97 (May 1901).

————. "The Rosary." *The Month* 96 (1900): 403–18, 513–27, 620–37; 97 (1901): 67–79, 172–88, 287–304, 383–404.

————. "Scapulars." *The Month* 149 (June 1927): 481–88, and 150 (June 1927): 44–58.

————. "The Stations of the Cross." *The Month* 96 (1900):1–12, 153–66, 282–93.

Vecoli, Rudolph. "Cult and Occult in Italian-American Culture: The Persistence of a Religious Heritage." In *Immigrants and Religion in Urban America*, pp. 25–47. Edited by Randall M. Miller and Thomas D. Marzik. Philadelphia: Temple University Press, 1977.

————. "Prelates and Peasants: Italian Immigrants and the Catholic Church." *Journal of Social History* 2 (1969):217–68.

Walker, Daniel P. *Unclean Spirits: Possession and Exorcism in France and England in the Late Sixteenth and Early Seventeenth Centuries.* Philadelphia: University of Pennsylvania Press, 1981.

Ward, Benedicta. *Miracles and the Medieval Mind.* Philadelphia: University of Pennsylvania Press, 1983.

Warner, Marina. *Alone of All Her Sex: The Myth and Cult of the Virgin Mary.* New York: Alfred A. Knopf, 1976.

Wolff, Bernice [Sister Mary Florence]. *The Sodality Movement in the United States, 1926–36.* St. Louis: The Queen's Work, 1939.

Woods, Ralph L. and Henry. *Pilgrim Places in North America.* New York and Toronto: Longman, Green and Co., 1939.

General

Addington, Raleigh, ed. *Faber, Poet and Priest: Selected Letters by Frederick William Faber, 1833–1863.* Cowbridge, England: D. Brown and Sons, 1974.

Aubert, Roger. *The Church in a Secularized Society.* New York: Paulist Press, 1978.

Baumgartner, Mildred Florence. *The Ave Maria Index, Vol. 1–25: May 1865–December 1887.* Notre Dame: University of Notre Dame [19–].

Berger, Peter. *Sacred Canopy: Elements of a Sociological Theory of Religion.* Garden City, N.Y.: Doubleday and Co., 1967; Anchor Books, 1969.

Bossy, John. "The Counter-Reformation and the People of Catholic Europe." *Past and Present* 47 (1970):53–70.

————. *The English Catholic Community, 1570–1850.* New York: Oxford University Press, 1976.

Brown, Peter. "Society and the Supernatural: A Medieval Change." *Daedalus* 104 (1975):133–51.

Brown, Thomas N. "The Origins and Character of Irish American Nationalism." *Review of Politics* 18 (1956): 327–58.

Browne, Henry J. "American Catholic History: A Progress Report on Research and Study." *Church History* 26 (1957): 372–80.

———. "The 'Italian Problem' in the Catholic Church of the United States." *Historical Records and Studies* 35 (1946): 46–72.

Burnaby, John. *Amor Dei: A Study of the Religion of St. Augustine.* London: Hodder and Stoughton, 1938.

Burton, Edwin H. *The Life and Times of Bishop Challoner, 1691–1781,* 2 vols. New York and London: Longmans, Green and Co., 1909.

Byrne, John F. *The Redemptorist Centenaries.* Philadelphia: The Dolphin Press, 1932.

Catholic University of America, Department of Library Science. *A Survey of Catholic Book Publishing in the United States, 1831–1900.* Eleven Master's theses on microfilm. Washington, D.C.: C.U.A. Photoduplication Service.

Chinnici, Joseph P. *The English Catholic Enlightenment: John Lingard and the Cisalpine Movement, 1780–1850.* Shepherdstown, W.Va.: Patmos Press, 1980.

———. "Politics and Theology: From Enlightenment Catholicism to the Condemnation of Americanism." Cushwa Center (University of Notre Dame), *Working Paper Series* 9/3 (Spring 1981).

Clark, Dennis J. "The Irish-Catholics: A Postponed Perspective." In *Immigrants and Religion in Urban America,* pp. 48–68. Edited by Randall M. Miller and Thomas D. Marzik. Philadelphia: Temple University Press, 1977.

———. *The Irish in Philadelphia: Ten Generations of Urban Experience.* Philadelphia: Temple University Press, 1973.

Cross, Robert D. *The Emergence of Liberal Catholicism in America.* Cambridge: Harvard University Press, 1958.

———. "The Origins of the Catholic Parochial Schools in America." *American Benedictine Review* 16 (1965): 194–200.

Curley, Michael J. *Venerable John Neumann, C.Ss.R., Fourth Bishop of Philadelphia.* Washington, D.C.: Catholic University of America, 1952.

Curran, Robert Emmett. "Prelude to Americanism: The New York Accademia and Clerical Radicalism in the Late Nineteenth Century." *Church History* 47 (1978): 45–65.

Davis, David Brion. "Some Themes of Counter-Subversion: An Analysis of Anti-Masonic, Anti-Catholic, and Anti-Mormon Literature." *Mississippi Valley Historical Review* 47 (1960):205–24.

Delumeau, Jean. *Catholicism Between Luther and Voltaire: A New View of The Counter-Reformation.* Introduction by John Bossy. Philadelphia: Westminster Press, 1977.

Dolan, Jay P. *The Immigrant Church: New York's Irish and German Catholics, 1815–1865.* Baltimore: Johns Hopkins University Press, 1977.

Dolan, Jay P., and Burns, Jeffrey. "The Parish History Project: A Descriptive Analysis of Data." Cushwa Center, University of Notre Dame, 1983 (typewritten).

Douglas, Mary. *Purity and Danger: An Analysis of the Concepts of Pollution and Taboo.* London and Henley: Routledge and Kegan Paul, 1966.

Dowling, Patrick John. *A History of Irish Education: A Study in Conflicting Loyalties.* Cork: Mercier Press, 1971.

Ebeling, Gerhard. *The Word of God and Tradition: Historical Studies Interpreting the Divisions of Christianity.* Translated by S. H. Hooke. London: William Collins Sons and Co., 1968.

Eisenstein, Elizabeth L. *The Printing Press as an Agent of Change: Communications and Cultural Transformations in Early-Modern Europe,* 2 vols. Cambridge: Cambridge University Press, 1979.

Elliott, Walter. *The Life of Father Hecker.* 2d ed. New York: Columbus Press, 1894.

Fennell, Desmond, ed. "The Myth of the Irish: A Failure of American Catholic Scholarship." In *The Changing Face of Catholic Ireland,* pp. 121–34. Compiled by Desmond Fennell. London: Geoffrey Chapman, 1968.

Finotti, Joseph M., Rev. *Bibliographia Catholica Americana: A List of Works Written By Catholic Authors, and Published in the United States.* 1871; reprint ed., New York: Burt Franklin, 1971.

Fogarty, Gerald P. "The Quest for a Catholic Vernacular Bible in America." In *The Bible in America: Essays in Cultural History,* pp. 163–80. Edited by Nathan O. Hatch and Mark A. Noll. New York and Oxford: Oxford University Press, 1983.

Fullam, Paul J. "The Catholic Publication Society and Its Successors, 1866–1916." *Historical Records and Studies* 47 (1959):12–77.

Garraghan, Gilbert J. *The Jesuits of the Middle United States,* 3 vols. New York: America Press, 1938.

Gaustad, Edwin Scott. *Historical Atlas of Religion in America*. New York: Harper and Row, 1962.

Gavigan, Kathleen. "The Rise and Fall of Parish Cohesiveness in Philadelphia." *Records of the American Catholic Historical Society* 86 (1975): 107–31.

Good, Patricia K. "Irish Adjustment to American Society: Integration or Separation? A Portrait of an Irish-Catholic Parish: 1863–1886." *Records of the American Catholic Historical Society* 86 (1975): 7–23.

Gordon, Milton. *Assimilation in American Life: The Role of Race, Religion and National Origins*. New York: Oxford University Press, 1964.

Graff, Harvey J. *The Literacy Myth: Literacy and Social Structure in the Nineteenth Century City*. New York: Academic Press, 1979.

Guilday, Peter. *A History of the Councils of Baltimore, 1791–1884*. New York: Macmillan Co., 1932.

Healey, Robert C. *A Catholic Book Chronicle: The Story of P. J. Kenedy and Sons, 1826–1951*. New York: P. J. Kenedy and Sons, 1951.

Hennesey, James. *American Catholics: A History of the Roman Catholic Community in the United States*. New York: Oxford University Press, 1981.

———. "Papacy and Episcopacy in Nineteenth Century American Thought." *Records of the American Catholic Historical Society of Philadelphia* 77 (1966): 175–89.

Holmes, Derek. *More Roman Than Rome: English Catholicism in the Nineteenth Century*. Shepherdstown, W.Va.: Patmos Press, 1978.

———. *The Triumph of the Holy See: A Short History of the Papacy in the Nineteenth Century*. Shepherdstown, W.Va.: Patmos Press, 1978.

Howlett, W. J. *Life of Rev. Charles Nerinckx: Pioneer Missionary and Founder of the Sisters of Loretto at the Foot of the Cross*. Techny, Ill.: The Mission Press, 1915.

Hueston, Robert Francis. *The Catholic Press and American Nativism, 1840–1860*. New York: Arno Press, 1976.

Kaestle, Carl F. *The Evolution of an Urban School System: New York City, 1750–1850*. Cambridge, Mass.: Harvard University Press, 1973.

———. *Pillars of the Republic: Common Schools and American Society, 1780–1860*. New York: Hill and Wang, 1983.

Kantowicz, Edward. "Church and Neighborhood." *Ethnicity* 7 (1980): 349–66.

Lazerson, Marvin. "Understanding American Catholic Educational History." *History of Education Quarterly* 17 (1977): 297–317.

Lees, Lynn Hollen. *Exiles of Erin: Irish Migrants in Victorian London.* Ithaca, N.Y.: Cornell University Press, 1979.

Light, Dale Beryl. "Class, Ethnicity, and the Urban Ecology in a Nineteenth Century City: Philadelphia's Irish, 1840–1890." Ph.D. dissertation, University of Pennsylvania, 1979.

McAvoy, Thomas T. "The Formation of the Catholic Minority in the United States, 1820–1860." *Review of Politics* 10 (1948): 13–34.

McLeod, Hugh. *Religion and the People of Western Europe, 1789–1970.* Oxford and New York: Oxford University Press, 1981.

McLoughlin, William G., Jr. *Modern Revivalism: Charles Grandison Finney to Billy Graham.* New York: Ronald Press, 1959.

McSweeney, William. *Roman Catholicism: The Search for Relevance.* New York: St. Martin's Press, 1980.

Maes, Camillus P. *The Life of Rev. Charles Nerinckx.* Cincinnati: Robert Clarke and Co., 1880.

Marty, Martin E. "The Catholic Ghetto and All the Other Ghettos." *Catholic Historical Review* 68 (1982): 184–205.

———. "Revival of Evangelicalism and Southern Religion." In *Varieties of Southern Evangelicalism*, pp. 7–21. Edited by David E. Harrell, Jr. Macon, Ga.: Mercer University Press, 1981.

Messbarger, Paul R. *Fiction with a Parochial Purpose: Social Uses of American Catholic Literature, 1884–1900.* Boston: Boston University Press, 1971.

Miller, David W. "Irish Catholicism and the Great Famine." *Journal of Social History* 9 (1975): 81–98.

Mulkerins, Thomas M. *Holy Family Parish, Chicago.* Edited and arranged by Joseph J. Thompson. Chicago: Universal Press, 1923.

Niehaus, Earl F. *The Irish in New Orleans, 1800–1860.* Baton Rouge: Louisiana State University Press, 1965.

Nolan, Hugh J. *The Most Reverend Francis Patrick Kenrick, Third Bishop of Philadelphia, 1830–1851.* Washington, D.C.: Catholic University of America Press, 1948.

O'Brien, David J. "American Catholic Historiography: A Post-Conciliar Evaluation." *Church History* 37 (1968): 80–94.

Parsons, Wilfrid. *Early Catholic Americana: A List of Books and Other*

Works by Catholic Authors in the United States, 1729–1830. New York: Macmillan Co., 1939.

Ricoeur, Paul. *Freud and Philosophy: An Essay in Interpretation.* Translated by Denis Savage. New Haven and London: Yale University Press, 1970.

———. *The Symbolism of Evil.* Boston: Beacon Press, 1967.

Ryan, Thomas Richard. *Orestes A. Brownson: A Definitive Biography.* Huntington, Ind.: Our Sunday Visitor, 1976.

Schultz, Stanley K. *The Culture Factory: Boston's Public Schools, 1789–1860.* New York: Oxford University Press, 1973.

Shannon, William V. *The American Irish.* Rev. ed. New York: Macmillan Co., 1966.

Sharp, John. "The Influence of St. Alphonsus Liguori in Nineteenth-Century Britain." *Downside Review* 101/342 (1983): 60–76.

Shaughnessy, Gerald. *Has the Immigrant Kept the Faith?* New York: Arno Press, 1969.

Skorupski, John. *Symbol and Theory: A Philosophical Study of Theories of Religion in Social Anthropology.* Cambridge: Cambridge University Press, 1976.

Smith, John Talbot. *The Catholic Church in New York: A History of the New York Diocese From its Establishment in 1808 to the Present Time.* New York and Boston: Hall and Locke, 1905.

Smith, Timothy L. "Protestant Schooling and American Nationality, 1800–1850." *Journal of American History* 53 (1967): 679–95.

Soltow, Lee, and Stevens, Edward. *The Rise of Literacy and the Common School in the United States: A Socioeconomic Analysis to 1870.* Chicago: University of Chicago Press, 1981.

Southern, Richard W. *Western Society and the Church in the Middle Ages.* New York: Penquin Books, 1970.

Spalding, Thomas W. *Martin John Spalding, American Churchman.* Washington, D.C.: Catholic University of America Press, 1973.

Spiro, Melford E. *Burmese Supernaturalism.* Expanded ed. Philadelphia: ISHI, 1978.

Sweeney, David Francis. "A Survey of Catholic Americana and Catholic Book Publishing in the United States, 1831–1840." M.A. thesis, Catholic University of America, 1950. In Catholic University of America, Department of Library Science. *A Survey of Catholic Book Publishing in the United States, 1831–1900.* Eleven Master's theses on microfilm. Washington, D.C.: C.U.A. Photoduplication Service.

Sweet, Leonard I., ed. *The Evangelical Tradition in America*. Macon, Ga.: Mercer University Press, 1984.

Swinburne, Richard, *The Concept of Miracle*. London: Macmillan and Co., 1970.

Tebbel, John William. *A History of Book Publishing in the United States*, 4 vols. New York: R. R. Bowker, 1972–1981.

Thernstrom, Stephan. *Poverty and Progress: Social Mobility in a Nineteenth Century City*. Cambridge, Mass.: Harvard University Press, 1964.

Tomasi, Sivano M. *Piety and Power: The Role of the Italian Parishes in the New York Metropolitan Area, 1880–1930*. New York: Center for Migration Studies, 1975.

Turner, Victor. *The Forest of Symbols: Aspects of Ndembu Ritual*. Ithaca and London: Cornell University Press, 1967.

Vecoli, Rudolph. "*Contadini* in Chicago: A Critique of *The Uprooted*." *Journal of American History* 51 (1961): 404–17.

Weber, Francis J. *America's Catholic Heritage: Some Bicentennial Reflections, 1776–1976*. [Boston]: St. Paul Editions, 1976.

Weber, Max. *The Sociology of Religion*. Translated by Ephraim Fischoff. Introduction by Talcott Parsons. Boston: Beacon Press, 1964.

Wright, John. *Early Prayer Books of America; Being a Descriptive Account of Prayer Books Published in the United States, Mexico and Canada*. St. Paul, Minn.: printed privately, 1896.

Yuhaus, Cassian J. *Compelled to Speak: The Passionists in America, Origin and Apostolate*. Westminster, Md.: Newman Press, 1976.

Index

Meditation: adapted for parish
missions, 73; and affective
bonds with supernatural beings, 74; and ethical action, 74,
79; structure of, 74–78
Men: in devotional organizations,
18; role of mother in devotional
life of, 83–87
Merits and satisfactions, 51
Messbarger, Paul, 54
Messenger of the Sacred Heart, The,
34, 55, 56, 63–65
Metaphors, devotional, 47. *See also*
Body; City; Family; Father;
Household; Mother
Milner, John (Bishop of Casta-
bala), 64
Miracles: and anti-Protestantism,
64; Catholic attitudes toward,
65–69, 162n.28; Protestant attitudes toward, 56–57, 64, 65; as
sanctions for devotions, 29, 30–
31, 38 (*see also* Visions); uses
of, 29, 63–65, 102
Miraculous cures, 56–63, 100; attitudes of sick toward, 68; and
international devotional organizations, 98; at shrines in the
U.S., 99
Miraculous medal, 36, 37, 39
Mission Book, The, 30, 43, 52, 53,
73, 74, 77
Missionary priests: and miraculous
cures, 60; paraliturgical practices, 2, 3, 34, 39; and parish
missions, 10. *See also* Faber,
Frederick William; Liguori, St.
Alphonsus
Months, devotions for particular,
25, 28. *See also* June; March;
May; October; November
Mother, as metaphor: for the
church, 110, 111; for Mary, 131
Mothers, and devotions, 83–87

Mulkerins, Bro. Thomas, 121
Murphy, John (Catholic publisher), 28

Nationalist organizations, Irish
American, 120
Nativism and American Catholics,
113, 127, 128
Nerinckx, Charles, 14–16
Neumann, John (Bishop of Philadelphia), 31
November, devotions to the souls
in purgatory for the month of,
25, 41, 121
Novenas, 25, 41; to the Immaculate Conception, 37, 121; and
miracles, 57, 60; to St. Joseph,
53, 123

October, rosary devotions for the
month of, 41
Original sin, and Mary, 108

Paraliturgical practices, 2, 23. *See
also* Devotions
Parents, natural and supernatural,
82–88
Parish missions: and conversion, 2;
and devotions, 2, 10–13, 33,
36, 39; English language, 11–
12; German language, 11–12;
at Holy Family parish, 121,
123; sermons and spiritual exercises, 73–74
Parish organizations, 16–17
Parishes: English-speaking, 17–19,
120–25; and generalized devotions, 120–25; German-speaking,
17–18
Parsons, Wilfrid, 5